From Beginning to Forever

A STUDY OF THE GRAND NARRATIVE OF SCRIPTURE

ELIZABETH WOODSON

Lifeway Press®
Brentwood, Tennessee

Published by Lifeway Press® • © 2022 Elizabeth Woodson

ISBN: 978-1-0877-6425-2 • Item: 005837658
Dewey decimal classification: 220.07
Subject heading: BIBLE—STUDY AND TEACHING / BIBLE—USE / PROVIDENCE AND GOVERNMENT OF GOD

To order additional copies of this resource, write to Lifeway Resources Customer Service; 200 Powell Place, Suite 100, Brentwood, TN, 37027-7707; order online at lifeway.com; fax 615.251.5933; phone toll free 800.458.2772; or email orderentry@lifeway.com.

Printed in the United States of America

Lifeway Women Bible Studies
Lifeway Resources
200 Powell Place, Suite 100,
Brentwood, TN, 37027-7707

EDITORIAL TEAM, LIFEWAY WOMEN BIBLE STUDIES

Becky Loyd
Director,
Lifeway Women

Tina Boesch
Manager

Chelsea Waack
Production Leader

Mike Wakefield
Content Editor

Erin Franklin
Production Editor

Lauren Ervin
Graphic Designer

CONTENTS

HOW TO USE THIS STUDY

Welcome to *From Beginning to Forever: A Study of the Grand Narrative of Scripture*. This is a study that will show you how all of Scripture is God's great story of redemption and restoration. Because we believe discipleship happens best in community, we encourage you to do this study together in a group setting. Or, if you're doing this alone, consider enlisting a friend or two to do it at the same time. This will give you study friends to pray with and connect with over coffee or through text or email so you can chat about what you're learning.

With the purchase of this Bible study book, you have access to teaching videos that provide content to help you better understand and apply what you just studied in the previous session. You'll find detailed information on how to **access the teaching videos** on the card inserted in the back of your Bible study book.

At times in the study, you'll be asked to look up Scripture passages in different translations. You can access those translations through biblegateway.com or other Bible apps. The various translations are abbreviated in the study:

AMP: Amplified Bible

CSB: Christian Standard Bible

ESV: English Standard Version

NIV: New International Version

NKJV: New King James Version

NLT: New Living Translation

WHAT'S INSIDE

Here are some things you're going to find in the study.

Video Guide: As you meet with your group each week, these pages provide a place to take notes from the video teaching and discussion questions to debrief the video teaching.

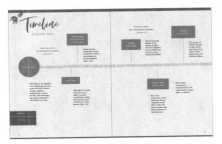

Time line: These pages give you a big-picture view of some of the events that took place during the Scripture passages covered in the week. They also show you the books of the Bible that relate to that time period or storyline.

Personal Study: Each week you'll have five days of personal study with the last day as a review day. In the sidebars beside words that are highlighted, you'll find "theological nuggets" that further explain the concept.

Leader Guide: This guide will help a leader prepare to lead the study and provide instruction for the content and flow of each group session.

ABOUT THE AUTHOR

Elizabeth Woodson is a Bible teacher and author who is passionate about equipping believers to understand the rich theological truths of Scripture. She loves helping people internalize their faith and connect it practically to everyday life.

She is a contributing author for *World on Fire* and the author of *Embrace Your Life: How To Find Joy When the Life You Have Is Not the Life You Hoped For*. She is also a graduate of Dallas Theological Seminary with a Masters in Christian Education.

A WORD FROM THE AUTHOR

For generations, we have communicated the truth about our existence from the perspective of a character in a narrative whose plotline is continually unfolding. As humans, we "have a built-in narrative instinct, as if we have been designed to use stories to remember our past, make sense of our present, and shape our future."[1] A collection of facts seen through the lens of our mind, body, and heart, stories are the means by which we interpret our life experiences. They help us make sense of the world and find our place within it, answering the three core life questions all of us ask—*Who am I? Why am I here? Where do I belong?*

However, we aren't born with these stories. Over the years, they are shaped by lots of different influences. The TV shows we watch, people we follow on social media, and our community all teach us how to view our lives and the world we live in.

Sometimes these stories teach us that we are what we have, look like, or do for a living. They encourage us to find our purpose in "following our hearts" or "doing what we feel." And most of all, they tell us that finding a place of belonging is easy—as long as we are doing the right thing to earn our spot!

While popular and enticing, these stories simply aren't true. In fact, only one can fully answer our core life questions—the story of the Bible! As the original and greatest Storyteller of all time, God gave us an epic story that explains who He is, who we are, and what He has for us to do in His world. It lays a foundation for us to build our lives upon and ultimately shows us that the good life can only be found in Jesus Christ!

Over the next eight sessions, you and I will walk through this story together.

When we jump into the beginning of the story, we will see in the first verses of the Bible that God's plan with creation was to establish His kingdom. But something went tragically wrong, and for the rest of Scripture, we will see God work to restore what He initiated at the beginning of time. With each session, we will take one more step toward the restoration of God's kingdom. The kingdom of God is where we are able to live the good life, and as we'll see in future weeks, it is the work of Jesus Christ that gets us into that kingdom.

We don't have time in this study to dig down deep into all the nitty-gritty details, so, we will examine the story from a fifty-thousand foot level, using the theme of kingdom to connect all the pieces of the story together. The goal of our journey will be to give you the tools to tell the story in your own words. Yes, YOU have the ability to not just know the story of the Bible but share it in your own words. We will work on your ability to retell the story a little bit each week, so by the end of the study you will have a summary of the entire story.

My hope is that by the end of this study you will understand how the entire story of Scripture helps us know who God is, who we are, and what we are called to do in His world. The goal, friends, is not to just know facts, but to study information that will transform our motivation for living and love for God.

I'm excited to jump into this journey with you!

Let's go!

Elizabeth

When we jump into the beginning of the story, we will see in the first verse of the Bible that God's plan with creation was to establish His kingdom. But something went tragically wrong, and for the rest of Scripture, we will see God work to restore what He initiated at the beginning of time.

SESSION ONE

Introduction

Video + Group Guide

SESSION ONE

WATCH Session One video teaching and take notes below.

To access the video teaching sessions, use the instructions in the back of your Bible study book.

DISCUSSION QUESTIONS

1   Why is "story" so important to our lives?

2   What currently has the biggest influence on your story?

3   Do you see the Bible as a collection of stories or one big story? Explain.

4   Before this teaching, how would you have explained the kingdom of God?

5   Do you now have a better understanding of kingdom? Explain.

6   What is one point or truth that really stood out to you from the video teaching? Why?

THE STATUS OF THE KINGDOM

In the chart below, write the definition of the kingdom of God. Then write in the explanation for each phrase I'll give you in the teaching video.

Definition of the Kingdom of God	Explanation
God's _____ in	
God's _____ under	
God's _____ and _____.	

SESSION TWO

The Creation & Corruption of the Kingdom

Timeline

SESSION TWO

ADAM AND EVE DRIVEN FROM EDEN

MEMORABLE WORDS
In the beginning God . . .
Genesis 1:1

CREATION

* God driving Adam and Eve from the garden of Eden was protection, not punishment (Gen. 3:22-23).

THE FALL

FUN FACT
The earth is an organism that reflects the creative power of God. It burns energy, regulates temperature, renews its skin, and undergoes age-related changes to its surface over time.[1]

* Although it's usually portrayed as an apple, we don't actually know what kind of fruit Adam and Eve ate in the garden (Gen. 3:6).

BOOKS

GENESIS

FUN FACT
The earth travels around the sun at 67,000 mph.

Am I my brother's keeper?

Genesis 4:9 (ESV)

TOWER OF BABEL

CAIN AND ABEL

* The devastating effects of sin appear quickly. Just four chapters into the Bible, we have a man killing his brother.

* The people of Babel's attempt to gain power apart from God mirrors what happened in the garden of Eden.

NOAH AND THE FLOOD

* The Noahic Covenant in Genesis 9:8-17 was sealed with a unique sign—a rainbow.

* Per God's instruction, Noah built the ark out of gopher wood (Gen. 6:14). Scholars are unsure what species of tree this is referring to.

Day 1

THE BEGINNING

If we were having coffee and I asked you to tell me about your day, most likely you would not give me a minute-by-minute breakdown of everything you had done. You would give me the highlights—the most important details to give me the best description of the story of your life that day.

The same is true for Scripture. The Bible is not an exhaustive history of the world. By the power of the Holy Spirit, the biblical authors only gave us the most important details, especially at the very beginning. Genesis 1 and 2 set the stage for the narrative of Scripture. Without fully understanding these two chapters, we cannot understand the rest of the Bible. While short in length, these two chapters contain vital information that creates a foundation for the entirety of Scripture.

The truth is, the whole of Scripture is preoccupied with trying to return to life with God as it was in the garden of Eden and the fulfillment of His garden plan for the world. If we don't see the story through this lens, we are going to pursue some lesser narrative. For example, we might reduce the Bible to a set of encouraging quotes or Christian living advice. While the Bible provides both encouragement and advice on how to live well as a Christian, it does so much more! Specifically, the creation account shows us what life on earth should look like. In other words, it shows us *shalom*—how we should live in community with God, each other, and all of creation.

Look up the word *shalom* in a dictionary and write a definition for it below.

shalom	

How does your definition compare to the current state of the world in which we live?

THEOLOGICAL NUGGET

SHALOM: A state of peace that refers to the total well-being of an individual or community. This emotional, physical, spiritual, and even financial wholeness is associated with God's presence among His people.[2]

READ REVELATION 21:3-4. How does your definition compare to the promised future state of the world?

In the first two chapters of Genesis, we are shown God's great goal for the world—His desire to live in community with humanity, ruling creation in a perfect environment of *shalom*.[1] This goal will frame how we understand the rest of Scripture. It will give us hope and also be our guide as we learn how the sixty-six books of the Bible combine to form one unified narrative.

Before we unpack the creation narrative, let's discuss a few important background details. As with any book of the Bible, in order for us to clearly understand what the author was writing about in Genesis, we first need to know who the author is, to whom he was writing, and the reason why he wrote the book.

READ DEUTERONOMY 31:7-9,24-26.

Who wrote the book of the Law? _____

To whom was it written? _____

The book of the Law does not just refer to the Ten Commandments but to the first five books of the Old Testament—Genesis, Exodus, Leviticus, Numbers, and Deuteronomy. Moses wrote these words after Israel was delivered out of Egypt. We will cover the details of Israel's story in Session Three, but with the opening words of Genesis, Israel was being introduced to the God who had rescued her out of slavery in Egypt. Through the hands of Moses, God showed the Israelites who He is, who they are, and what their purpose is in the world.

Now that we've laid a foundation for the beginning of the story, let's jump in!

Let's start with the first verse of the Bible, Genesis 1:1. Write it out.

Based on this verse, who is the main character of the Bible?

Why is this important for us to remember as we read through the Bible?

READ GENESIS 1:1–2:3 and fill in the table to summarize God's creation of the world.

Day	Scripture Reference	What did God create?
Day 1	Genesis 1:2-5	
Day 2		
Day 3		
Day 4		
Day 5		
Day 6		

What three things did God do on the seventh day of creation
(Gen. 2:3)?

1.

2.

3.

Since God is not human, He does not get tired as we do. Why did He
choose to "rest" on the seventh day? Give your best answer; we will
cover it in the video teaching time.

Genesis 1 and 2 both describe the same events but do so differently. One creation
account is more poetic, while the other uses more prose. Either way, in the first two
pages of Scripture, God detailed the establishment of His kingdom. We see Him
create a world in which all of humanity and creation thrive under His loving care. It
is a world that embodies *shalom*, where everything is as it should be.

Look back to your notes on page 13 and write below the definition of
the kingdom of God.

God's _____ *in God's* _____ *under*

God's _____ *and* _____.[3]

Summarize what you learned about the kingdom of God in Genesis 1 and 2 by answering the following questions.

1. Who are the people God created? _____
   and _____

2. Describe the place God created for them to live. Include details about the two trees that were in this place.

3. What rules did God give them (Gen. 2:16-17)? How would their obedience to these rules result in blessing?

While lots of questions can arise concerning the specific details of creation, it's helpful for us to focus on the author's main points—God created, creation is good, and humanity is unique among creation. The beginning of the story matters, and in the first two chapters of the Bible, we are introduced to God's divine design for all of creation. Tomorrow we are going to dig a little deeper into the story, examining what it tells us about God and ourselves.

Day 2

IMAGE BEARERS

At some point, all of us will ask ourselves three important questions: *Who am I? Where do I belong? What am I here for?* Innate within our humanity is a longing for identity, community, and purpose. Yet whether through social media, the latest self-help guru, or a close friend, many of us will try to find answers to these questions outside of the Bible. While we view the Bible as providing helpful advice, we fail to see it as what it is—the primary influence of our worldview, shaping how we view ourselves and the world we live in.

In its first few pages, the Bible provides us with answers to our questions of identity, community, and purpose. Through the words of Moses, God was showing Israel and us that our best lives are lived in community with Him and His people, under His rule and blessing. By showing us who He is, we are able to understand who we are called to be and what we are called to do in His world.

In the words of the theologian John Calvin, "without knowledge of God there is no knowledge of self."[4] Before we can fully understand who we are, we have to first understand who God is, specifically what He has revealed about Himself in Scripture. So, let's look back over Genesis 1 and 2 and see what these passages teach us about God.

> **READ GENESIS 1:1.** Fill in the blanks below to complete the first four words of this verse.
>
> _____ the _____ _____
>
> Is the word you used to fill in the last blank singular or plural? Why is this significant? What does this one detail teach us about God?

Remember, Moses was writing Genesis to the Israelites after they had been delivered out of Egypt. The Israelites had been under Egyptian rule as slaves for four hundred years. This means they would have been very familiar with, and perhaps even influenced by, the Egyptians' religious practices, maybe even more so than the God of the Bible.[5]

READ EXODUS 12:12.

What is the main difference between the gods the Egyptians worshiped and the God of the Bible?

In light of your answer, why do you think the words of Genesis 1:1 would have been especially significant for Israel?

God's first description of Himself shows He alone is God. No other being, animal, or part of nature rivals His authority; He alone is sovereign.

Look up the word *sovereign* in a dictionary and write a definition for it.

In Genesis 1, what repeated phrase did Moses use to describe how God created the world? Read Psalm 33:6 to help with your answer.

The first demonstration of God's sovereignty takes place within creation. The magnitude of God's power is demonstrated by how He creates all things by His word.[6] Not only did God create by His word, His word created out of nothing! Only God has the power to do this, and therefore, in the first sentence of the Bible, He established Himself as the One who has full control and authority over all of creation. Since He created the world, He alone gets to determine how His creation lives.

READ PSALM 95:1-7. How should we respond to God's sovereignty?

Now that we have learned what the creation narrative tells us about God, let's see what it tells us about our divine identity and purpose.

Genesis 1:26-27 tells us we are made in God's image.

With what other part of creation do we share this aspect? How should this impact how we view ourselves?

Some words carry a consistent meaning throughout time while others have a specific meaning that is connected to a specific point in time. This is true for the word *image*. In ancient Near Eastern culture, which is the culture of the original audience of Genesis, kings would leave images of themselves in the cities or areas they ruled.[7] These "images" were designed to remind the people of the power and grandeur of the king.

In Daniel 3, King Nebuchadnezzar of Babylon built a ninety-foot tall statue that the people were to bow down and worship.[8] As Nebuchadnezzar's *image* was built to represent him, in similar fashion we were designed to represent God. But instead of reflecting the oversized ego of an arrogant king, we were designed to reflect the good and true attributes of God to the world. By interacting with us or seeing how we interact with others, people should be able to know what God is like.

In Galatians 5:22-23, Paul listed the fruit of the Spirit—attributes of God—that we should embody as His children: love, joy, peace, patience, kindness, goodness, faithfulness, gentleness, and self-control.

God's attributes fall into two different categories, communicable and incommunicable. His communicable attributes are those we can embody as His creation, such as love, joy, peace, and patience. His incommunicable attributes are those that He alone can display, such as omnipotence, omnipresence, and omniscience.

CULTURAL MANDATE is the term theologians use to describe the divine purpose we have been given in Genesis 1:28.

Choose two of the attributes and list ways you can exhibit those characteristics at work, home, or school this week.

In addition to our divine design as image bearers, the creation narrative also shows us our divine purpose.

LOOK UP GENESIS 1:28 IN THE NEW LIVING TRANSLATION (NLT). What words are used in place of *subdue* and *rule* (or *have dominion over*)?
_____ and _____

What do these words illustrate about how humanity is supposed to care for the rest of God's creation?

VICE-REGENT: a person who acts in place of a ruler, governor, or sovereign

As King, God has given us the responsibility to steward His creation, helping it to flourish. We have been given the royal role of vice-regents, representing God's reign over creation and exercising dominion on His behalf. To echo the words of Jesus in Matthew 6:10, our kingdom task is to ensure that God's will is done on earth as it is in heaven.[9] Nothing we do is mundane or ordinary; rather it is an opportunity to help God's creation flourish and thrive!

Think about the current responsibilities you have in your sphere of influence (for example, work, home, or school). How would you approach these responsibilities differently if you saw them through the lens of your divine purpose?

The answers to our questions about identity, purpose, and belonging are found within the opening pages of Scripture. We serve a sovereign God, who alone holds all authority as King. He has made us in His image and given us the responsibility to cultivate the world He created; our best life is found in community with God. But as we will see tomorrow, when we try to find the answers to these questions outside of God, things quickly take a turn for the worst.

Day 3

REBELLION

On Day One of this study, we discussed how the biblical authors didn't give us every detail—only the most important ones. So, as we walk through the biblical narrative, we need to pay attention to the information these authors share with us as well as how they share it.

One important detail I want us to focus on today is the order in which the biblical authors chose to tell the story of how the world began. The order is significant because the Bible starts with Genesis 1, not Genesis 3. In the words of Michael Williams, "If we miss the biblical emphasis upon the goodness of God's original creation, we will also fail to see the blasphemy of sin for what it truly is: a rebellion against God and his good gifts, a rebellion from the loving word of God, a rebellion that brings discord and fracture into God's creation. Sin is never normal or natural. It never fits."[10]

READ GENESIS 3:1-7.

Then reread verse 1 in different translations—the Christian Standard Bible (CSB), New International Version (NIV), and New Living Translation (NLT). Compare the word each translation uses to describe the serpent. What insight into the serpent's character do these words provide?

Why did the biblical author include this detail for his readers at the beginning of the story?

How did the serpent's question to Eve distort the words God gave in Genesis 2:16-17?

Living up to his character, the serpent asked Eve a strategic question that intentionally drew her attention away from the blessings of God, casting doubt about His sufficiency and goodness. Instead of highlighting the vast provision that God had given them, the serpent focused on the one prohibition.

> What did the serpent say would happen if Adam and Eve ate the fruit (Gen. 3:4)? How did his words cast doubt on God's character?

> Based upon what we read in Genesis 1–2, how do we know that what the serpent said is untrue? Give your best answer; we will cover it in the video teaching time.

> In Genesis 3:6, the biblical author gave three reasons why Eve ate the fruit. List them below.

> 1.

> 2.

> 3.

Unfortunately, Adam and Eve chose to trust the serpent over God, eating the forbidden fruit. Instead of trusting God as their King and following the rules He set up for how they should live in the garden, they trusted their own judgment. Instead of believing that God's way was good, they believed their way was better and in doing so chose to be king of their own lives. Instead of living under God's authority as His image bearers and royal stewards of His world, they wanted to live under their own authority. This one act of disobedience introduced sin into the world.

> According to our culture, is sin a serious offense? List two words or phrases people in our culture might use to describe sin.

Look up the verses below and write the word(s) used to describe sin.

Exodus 23:21 _____

Leviticus 26:40 _____

Judges 2:11 _____

1 John 3:4-5 _____

According to Scripture, is sin a serious offense? Explain why.

Sin is described as any thought, word, or action that does not conform to God's instructions in the Bible.[11] As the Creator of the universe, God is perfect in all His ways. He is perfectly good, perfectly wise, perfectly holy, and so much more. God always knows what's best, so when we choose our way over His, it's because we believe that something or someone is more trustworthy than Him.

Why is it sometimes hard for us to trust that God's way is best?

What sins do you struggle with? What or who are you choosing to trust in rather than trusting in the character of God (for example, friends, self, or material objects that bring you joy or comfort)?

The impact of Adam and Eve's actions was immediate. Instantaneously, their sinful choice gave them knowledge of good and evil, but not in the way they expected.

Use the table below to summarize how Adam and Eve's decision changed their lives.

	BEFORE ADAM AND EVE EAT THE FRUIT	AFTER ADAM AND EVE EAT THE FRUIT
Their view of their bodies	Genesis 2:25	Genesis 3:7
Their relationship with God	Genesis 2:7,15-21	Genesis 3:8-10
Their relationship with each other	Genesis 2:21-24	Genesis 3:11-12

Adam and Eve were created to live in a perfect world, in relationships with God and one another that were without strife, selfishness, and shame. But sin changed everything, both with creation and humanity. The environment of *shalom* was now broken, and that brokenness would affect humanity at its very core. You see, Adam and Eve's actions didn't impact only them. Before they ate the fruit, Adam and Eve were able to not sin. But after they ate the fruit, sin became the default setting for them and all of humanity. Romans 5:12 tells us that "just as sin entered the world through one man, and death through sin, in this way death spread to all people, because all sinned."

However, sin doesn't only affect us individually. It also affects us corporately. When sinful people come together, they create institutions and systems that allow sinful behavior to be promoted throughout the culture. Actions and issues like abortion, racism, human trafficking, and other injustices are a few examples of what results when a group of image bearers create systems that harm other image bearers.

READ AMOS 5:11-12.

In this passage, the prophet Amos addressed the nation of Israel.
What was Israel guilty of doing?

Why is it easier for us to focus more on individual sin than corporate sin?

How should God's view of Israel's behavior impact how we view
corporate sin in our culture?

When sin entered the world, our ability to live in fellowship with God, perfectly
living out our divine calling as image bearers, died. Instead of building God's
kingdom, humanity now seeks to build its own rival kingdom. Instead of living
under God's authority, we fight to live under our own. As we walk through the
story, we will see this cosmic war between the kingdom of God and the kingdom
of this world unfold. But no matter how bad things get, there is always hope! No
one is more powerful than our God, and tomorrow we will see the first glimpse of
how our great and mighty God will conquer sin and restore His kingdom.

Day 4

THE PROMISE

With one decision, Adam and Eve's lives immediately changed. Their desire for autonomy resulted in an act of cosmic rebellion. God made them to be rulers, but they were not content being rulers. They wanted to be king and queen. They wanted to be their own authority, not live under the authority of God. Among the trees in the garden was a tree of life and a tree of the knowledge of good and evil that resulted in death. Adam and Eve chose the latter and would now experience the consequences of their decision, which would include being sent away from Eden and separated from the presence of God.[12]

COMPARE GENESIS 3:14-19 IN THE NIV AND NLT. In your own words, summarize the curses that God gave the serpent, Eve, and Adam.

THE SERPENT

1.

2.

3.

EVE

1.

2.

```
┌─────────────────────────────────────────────┐
│  ADAM                                         │
│                                               │
│     1.                                        │
│                                               │
│     2.                                        │
│                                               │
└─────────────────────────────────────────────┘
```

At the end of this very sad scene, God shed the blood of animals to provide a more permanent solution for Adam and Eve's inadequate fig leaf coverings. In the midst of His judgment, He showed them love and compassion. Proverbs 3:11-12 says, "Do not despise the LORD's instruction, my son, and do not loathe his discipline; for the LORD disciplines the one he loves, just as a father disciplines the son in whom he delights." God knew what Adam and Eve's future would be like and what they would need. Instead of letting them leave ill-prepared, He blessed them.

Why did God send Adam and Eve away from the garden (Gen. 3:22-23)?

Because of their disobedience, Adam and Eve were now living in a sinful state. God could not allow them to eat from the tree of life and live forever in that condition, so He sent them away from the garden of Eden. They were separated from the presence of God, their only Source of peace and wholeness. Being cast out of the garden was also indicative of the broken relationship they had with Him, as they now lived as enemies of God (Rom. 5:10). But even though the end of Adam and Eve's story in Genesis 3 might look bleak, God did not leave them (and us) without hope! Before He sent Adam and Eve on their way, God made a huge promise that one day He would fix what they broke. Let's go back to Genesis 3:15 and take a look at it.

READ GENESIS 3:15 IN VARIOUS TRANSLATIONS.

In your own words, summarize what God said to the serpent.

Describe the difference between the impact delivered by the offspring and the impact delivered by the serpent. Who will win this promised battle of hostility?

What does this promise teach us about God's character? In the moments you are struggling with sin, how can this truth provide you with hope and encouragement?

As we read through the narrative of Scripture, we will see God pursuing His people despite their continual rejection of His love and authority. After Adam and Eve ate the fruit, God could have chosen to wipe out the entire world and start over again. But He didn't. Instead of discarding His broken image bearers, God worked over hundreds of years to save them. Through Christ, God has done what we cannot—overcome sin (2 Cor. 5:21)! No matter how bad things get, we'll see that God is always working to fulfill the promise He made in Genesis 3:15.

After Adam and Eve left the garden, things went downhill quickly. The power of sin quickly became evident, as well as the speed by which it overtook humanity. From Genesis 4–11, the biblical author shows us how quickly sin spreads. Starting with the serpent's evil promise of autonomy, it quickly moves to a full-blown culture of godlessness where all of humanity has come together in the ultimate act of rebellion—the elevation of their own authority over God's authority.[13]

READ GENESIS 4:1-16 and fill in the chart to summarize what you learn.

	Abel	Cain
What was his vocation?		
What did each present as an offering to the Lord?		
How did God respond to each offering?		

What warning did God give Cain in verse 7? Did Cain heed this warning? Why or why not?

Despite Cain's actions, in what way did God show him grace (Gen. 4:11-15)?

We are only four chapters into the narrative of Scripture, and there has been a murder. Things escalated quickly after what happened in the garden. Unfortunately, the spread of sin did not slow down; it only became more and more pervasive. Whether it's the story of Noah in Genesis 5–10 or the story of the Tower of Babel in Genesis 11, humanity quickly started to build their own kingdom. But instead of being rooted in the goal of stewardship, flourishing, and *shalom*, they were rooted in selfishness, self-preservation, and self-exaltation.

Through these stories, the biblical author is showing us the vast impact of sin, how it breeds corruption and therefore demands God's judgment. But through these same stories, we also see that God's judgment is never an end in itself but rather a means to restore *shalom*. God will not allow the sin of man to undo the creation order or thwart His redemptive purposes.[14]

Day 5

WEEKLY REVIEW

On Day Five of each session, we will spend time reviewing what you've experienced over the past four days. This gives you time to both catch up and reflect on what you have learned.

This review process will be twofold.

1. I will ask you to answer a series of questions that will help you summarize the main points of that session's lesson.

2. After you complete the questions, use your answers to write a two to three sentence summary for what happened in the grand narrative of Scripture that session.

This session we walked through the first part of the grand narrative of Scripture—the creation and the fall of the kingdom. Answer the questions to summarize this session's main points. Feel free to use bullet points.

1. What are some things God created?

2. What does God's creative act teach us about Him?

3. What divine identity and purpose does God give humanity?

4. What happened when Adam and Eve ate the fruit?

5. What were the long-lasting kingdom consequences of this decision?

6. How did God promise to restore the kingdom?

SUMMARIZE THE NARRATIVE

In the space below, use your answers to the previous questions to create a two to three sentence summary of what happened this session in the grand narrative of Scripture.

Video + Group Guide

SESSION TWO

WATCH Session Two video teaching and take notes below.

To access the video teaching sessions, use the instructions in the back of your Bible study book.

DISCUSSION QUESTIONS

1   How would you define *shalom*?

2   Why is it so important for us to understand how the story of Scripture begins?

3   What do we learn about God from the creation story?

4   What do we learn about ourselves from the creation story?

5   What's significant about God's story starting in Genesis 1 rather than Genesis 3?

6   What is one point or truth that really stood out to you from the video teaching? Why?

THE STATUS OF THE KINGDOM

In the chart below, fill in the blanks to review the definition of the kingdom of God. (Look back at your notes on p. 13 if you need help). At the close of each teaching video, I will update the status of each phrase.

The Kingdom of God	Creation of the Kingdom	Corruption of the Kingdom
God's _____ in		
God's _____ under		
God's _____ and _____.		

SESSION THREE

A Promise to Restore the Kingdom

Timeline

SESSION THREE

GOD CALLS ABRAHAM

* Several scholars believe that the migration of the patriarchs (Abraham, Isaac, and Jacob) took place during the Middle Bronze Age (2000–1550 BC).[1]

JACOB AND ESAU

2000 BC   1900 BC   1800 BC   1700 BC

ISAAC IS BORN

JOSEPH

"The LORD was with Joseph."
Genesis 39:2,21,23

* There was a lot of laughter around Isaac's birth. Abraham laughed (Gen. 17:17). Sarah laughed (Gen. 18:12). It's only fitting they named their son Isaac, meaning "laughter."[2]

BOOKS

GENESIS

EXODUS

LEVITICUS

NUMBERS

DEUTERONOMY

Hear, O Israel: The LORD
our God, the LORD is one.
Deuteronomy 6:4 (ESV)

THE TEN COMMANDMENTS

1. No other gods.
2. No idols.
3. Don't misuse God's name.
4. Keep the Sabbath holy.
5. Honor your father and mother.
6. Don't murder.
7. Don't commit adultery.
8. Don't steal.
9. Don't give false testimony.
10. Don't covet.

ISRAELITES ENSLAVED IN EGYPT

* The Israelites were enslaved in Egypt for approximately four hundred years.

| 1600 BC | 1500 BC | 1400 BC | 1300 BC | 1200 BC |

Let my
people go.
Exodus 5:1

MOSES LEADS THE ISRAELITES OUT OF EGYPT

THE TEN PLAGUES

1. Water to blood
2. Frogs
3. Gnats
4. Flies
5. Death of livestock
6. Boils
7. Hail
8. Locusts
9. Darkness
10. Death of firstborn

* **Manna:** grainlike food that God provided for the Israelites to eat while wandering in the wilderness. They ground it and either baked it or boiled it (Ex. 16:13-36).

Day 1

A NEW BEGINNING

In the first eleven chapters of Genesis, we see the beauty of God's creation quickly disrupted. Once sin was introduced into the world, it spread, causing death and depravity that culminated in worldwide rebellion against God. Those who were designed to live in community with God, building His kingdom, decided they wanted to build a kingdom for themselves. But in epic fashion, God responded by scattering the nations throughout the earth (Gen. 11:1-9).

In Genesis 3:15, God made a promise to restore His kingdom. He promised that one day the head of the serpent, which represents Satan and sin itself, would be crushed and permanently eradicated from the world. One day, all that is broken would be made whole. But by the end of Genesis 11, the corruption of the kingdom had not been remedied. Sin still existed, and humanity was living in rebellion, fully opposed to God.

As we read through Scripture, we are going to keep asking the same question—*How would God keep His promise?* Through each book of the Bible, we will look for the ways in which God was keeping the promise He made in Genesis!

This session, we will get one of our first answers in Genesis 12.

Let's jump in!

READ GENESIS 12:1. To whom was God speaking in this verse?

The story of the Tower of Babel ends with the focus on the whole world, but in Genesis 12, the story narrows to one man and his family line. In these first few verses of chapter 12, we see God singled out Abraham (God changed Abram's name to Abraham in Gen. 17:5)—descended from Noah's son, Shem, fathered by Terah, and married to Sarai, who was barren. Terah moved the family from Ur of the Chaldeans and headed to Canaan, but they didn't make it that far. Instead, they settled in Haran (Gen. 11:26-31). From there in Haran, God called

Abraham out for a special purpose and made a series of promises that combined to form one large promise called a *covenant*.

Look up the word *covenant* in a dictionary. In your own words, write a definition for it below.

covenant

ADAMIC COVENANT

Genesis 1–3

NOAHIC COVENANT

Genesis 6–9

ABRAHAMIC COVENANT

Genesis 12; 15; 17

MOSAIC COVENANT

Exodus 19–24

DAVIDIC COVENANT

2 Samuel 7

The word *covenant* is not widely used today. For most of us, the only covenant we have heard of is a marriage covenant. But in the ancient near east, covenants were more commonplace. During the time of Abraham, kings would make covenants with their subjects that specified requirements for each party in the agreement. These contracts were binding, so to break them was a big deal, which usually resulted in a harsh penalty.

In the Bible, covenants are the major thread that connect the sixty-six books of the Bible into one unified story. As we read through Scripture, we will see God make several covenants that were all rooted in His plan to redeem humanity and restore His kingdom: the Noahic Covenant, Abrahamic Covenant, Mosaic Covenant, Davidic Covenant, and the New Covenant. These covenants are progressive, which means they build upon each other, and all of them are fulfilled in Jesus Christ. But I'm getting a little ahead of myself. Before we get to Jesus, we have to talk about Abraham and a few other folks!

God's covenant with Abraham unfolds in Genesis 12; 15; 17. We will focus on the promises Abraham was given in Genesis 12:1-3 and then look at the other two chapters to see how they expand upon the promise.

READ GENESIS 12:1-3. What three things did God tell Abraham to leave behind?

1.
2.
3.

Where did He tell him to go? _____

What promises did God make to Abraham?

1. I will _____.

2. I will _____.

3. I will _____.

4. You will _____.

5. I will _____.

6. I will _____.

7. All the peoples on earth will _____.

In these three verses, God made a promise to Abraham about Abraham's future. If Abraham would obediently follow after God, God would give him three things—land, people, and blessing. Through Abraham, God would restore His kingdom, establishing a place for His people under His rule and blessing.

What was the name of the land God promised to give Abraham (Gen. 12:4-7)?

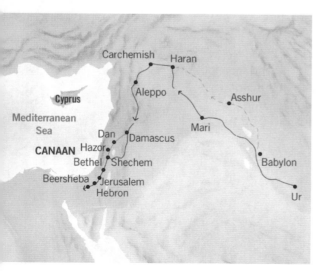

Who else lived in this land? Why do you think God promised to give Abraham a place that was occupied by other people?

Look at the map that shows where God sent Abraham. Circle each stop Abraham made along the way of his journey (Gen. 12:4-9).

Where did Abraham eventually end up settling?

Why do you think he was not able to immediately take hold of the land that had been promised to him?

Many of the promises God made in Scripture were not immediately fulfilled. While God showed His people in advance how He would rescue them, His plan of redemption unfolded over generations. The people of God had to patiently wait and trust that God would make good on His promises.

Describe a situation where you had to wait on God to fulfill a promise in your life. Was it easy or difficult for you to patiently wait on God? Explain your answer.

What did you learn about God and yourself during this time of waiting?

As believers, what can we do to increase our trust in God, even when it doesn't look like He is going to come through? Read Psalm 9:10 and Isaiah 41:10 to help you with your answer.

The covenant God made with Abraham also included a promise about who would live in the land God would give him.

READ GENESIS 15:1-6 AND GENESIS 17:1-8. In your own words, describe what God meant when He said He would make Abraham "a great nation" (Gen. 12:2).

LOOK BACK TO GENESIS 11:30. What unique detail from the biblical author makes God's promise of offspring seem unrealistic? What does this dynamic show us about God?

The final part of God's covenant with Abraham included a promise of blessing. The blessing God gave Abraham was twofold, for Abraham both received blessing from God and brought blessing to the entire world.

Covenants were usually finalized through a special ceremony that included animal sacrifice. The animals would be cut in half and laid on the ground with space for both parties to walk in-between. As they passed between the animal pieces, both parties were acknowledging that whoever failed to uphold their end of the agreement would meet the same fate the animals had. In Genesis 15, God participated in this type of ceremony with Abraham. But only God passed between the pieces, symbolizing that the fulfillment of the covenant depended on Him alone. While Abraham had to be obedient to the covenant in order to experience blessing, we see that God remained faithful and committed to His goal of kingdom restoration no matter what happened!

Today we saw how God chose Abraham and his descendants to be His people. In His sovereignty, He singled out this one man and his family to serve as the conduit through which He would redeem humanity and restore His kingdom. They were God's people, under His rule and blessing, on their way to a place God set apart for them. God's kingdom restoration plan had been set in motion!

Tomorrow we will learn that no matter the obstacle, nothing will thwart God's plan to make Abraham a great nation.

Day 2

ABRAHAM AND SONS

God chose to restore His kingdom through Abraham and his family, promising to use them to bring blessing to the entire world. However, there were two small problems—Abraham didn't have any children, and his wife was barren. Of all the people in the world to choose, God decided to work through a husband and wife who struggled with infertility. But what seemed like an impossible situation was an opportunity for God to show His power and faithfulness. His covenant with Abraham included both physical fruitfulness and blessing for Abraham's offspring. Today we will see how God's favor overcame a barren womb and continued to follow His chosen people, even when they believed He had forgotten them.

READ GENESIS 16:1-6.

What problem did Abraham and Sarah claim to have, and how did they try to solve it?

Describe what happened when they tried to fulfill God's promise on their own.

Waiting is hard, and after a long time of waiting on God, Abraham and Sarah decided to do what many of us try to do—help God out! But instead of making the situation better, their solution caused division in their home. What amazes me about this story is how God responded to Hagar. After Sarah kicked her out of the home, God met Hagar with kindness and compassion. He told her to go back and submit to Sarah and then promised her she would give birth to a son,

Ishmael (Gen. 16:11). He even promised to bless her by multiplying her offspring, so much so that there would "be too many to count" (Gen. 16:10).

In Genesis 16:13, what name did Hagar give God, and what does the name mean?

How have you seen God show up in the same way in your life? Give one example.

Not only did God show favor to Hagar, but He also showed favor to Abraham. Instead of abandoning him or harshly judging him for his disbelief, God showed him compassion. In Genesis 17, God reaffirmed His covenant with Abraham, revealing that regardless of Abraham's unfaithfulness, God would be faithful to fulfill what He had promised.

What two commands did God give Abraham in Genesis 17:1,9?

What additional detail did God provide about the status of who would be included in Abraham and Sarah's descendants (Gen. 17:6,16)? Why is this significant? Give your best answer; we will cover it in the video teaching time.

In Genesis 17:9-14, God used the sign of circumcision to represent the covenant between Him and Abraham (and Abraham's future generations). After affirming the covenant with Abraham, God pronounced future blessing for Abraham's son Ishmael and his future son, Isaac. Both would become great nations, but only through Isaac would the covenant be honored.

Even though Abraham and Sarah tried to remedy their situation on their own, God was resolute in His efforts to honor the promise He made to them. Fourteen years after the birth of Ishmael, Sarah gave birth to Isaac. I can't imagine the joy Sarah must have felt seeing the faithfulness of God after such a long time of waiting. The hope for their future legacy had finally been born!

Genesis 25–36 continues the story of blessing for Abraham and his family. In these chapters, we read the stories of Abraham's son, grandson, and great-grandsons. In their journeys, we will see commonalities—God's provision and protection for them, their unfaithfulness to God, and God's reaffirmation of the covenant He made with Abraham that would continue to be fulfilled through them.

READ GENESIS 25:19-26. What problem did Rebekah have? Who else had this same problem in the Scripture we've read?

How did God graciously resolve the situation?

After the birth of Isaac's sons Jacob and Esau, God reaffirmed the covenant He made with Abraham.

READ GENESIS 26:1-6 and draw a line from the promise to the correct Scripture reference.

People	Genesis 26:3
Land	Genesis 26:4a
Blessing	Genesis 26:4b

God spoke these words of affirmation right before Isaac was about to enter into a situation where he would need to trust God for protection. Because of a famine, he had to move into a land that was occupied by the Philistines, and he was scared of them. Isaac was under the care of a God who had shown Himself faithful to Isaac and his father. But like many of us in situations of crisis, it can be easy to rely on our own strength instead of waiting for the provision of God.

So, instead of trusting God to protect them, he employed his father's strategy and told the king that Rebekah was his sister and not his wife (Gen. 26:7-11). Despite both men's unfaithfulness, God showered them both with immense blessing, so much so that the very person they feared, King Abimelech, agreed to a permanent treaty of peace.

As this highlight of God's provision and care for Isaac comes to a close, the focus of the narrative moves to his two sons, Jacob and Esau.

We can go back one chapter in Genesis to get some background information about both men. In Genesis 25:19-26, we find out that Rebekah was pregnant with twins who "struggled with each other" while in the womb (v. 22). When she asked the Lord the reason for this, He told her she had "two nations" in her womb and they would be divided, with the younger child leading a people who would be stronger than the older child's people (v. 23). Fittingly, when the children were born, the younger child, Jacob, was grasping the heel of Esau, the older child.

In the time of Abraham, the birthright was a group of special privileges that belonged to the firstborn male child in a family.[1] One significant privilege was a double portion of the father's estate as an inheritance. For instance, if a man had two sons, his estate would be divided into three portions, and his older son would receive two. In addition, during a father's final few moments of life, he would bestow a blessing on his children, with the eldest child usually receiving the greatest blessing.

What happened to Esau's birthright in Genesis 25:29-34?

Describe the difference between the blessing Isaac gave Jacob and the one he gave Esau in Genesis 27:27-40. Who received the greater blessing? Explain why.

The events involving the blessing and birthright were a fulfillment of what God promised in Genesis 25:21-23 and illustrated an important truth—God works in unexpected ways to accomplish His mission of kingdom restoration. If we read the story of Jacob and Esau logically, we would have expected God to choose to work through Esau, but He chose Jacob. Now, let's be honest, Jacob was not chosen because he was virtuous but because of God's grace.[2] For a reason only known to Him, God would now work to fulfill His promise to Abraham through Jacob.

How has God worked in unexpected ways in your life? Share an example.

Why is it important for us to remember that God often works in ways we do not expect or even understand?

Today we saw God work in unexpected ways to fulfill His promises. Whether it was opening the wombs of barren women or choosing a man whose character is less than stellar, God remained faithful to the covenant He made with Abraham.

Tomorrow we will learn more about Jacob and how God quickly expanded his family from twelve sons to a nation of hundreds of thousands of people!

Day 3

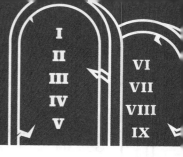

JACOB AND SONS

God promised Abraham he would be the father of many nations, but at this point in the story, the nations only included his sons, Isaac and Ishmael, and his grandson, Jacob. We've got a ways to go before this blessing would be fulfilled. But as we follow the life of Jacob, we will see how God continued to expand the family line and protect the offspring of Abraham no matter what they faced. Nothing and no one thwarts the plans of God!

As we jump back into the story, Jacob's deceitful behavior resulted in him having to flee his homeland Beersheba and go to Haran to be with his mother's brother, Laban (Gen. 27). After Jacob arrived in Haran, he met and immediately fell in love with Laban's daughter Rachel. But Laban deceived Jacob so that Jacob ended up marrying Laban's first daughter Leah before he married Rachel. After both marriages took place, God opened Leah's womb, and she quickly began having children, but Rachel, like Jacob's mother and grandmother, was unable to conceive.

God eventually opened up Rachel's womb and allowed her to bear two children, Joseph and Benjamin. As a result of Laban's deceptive behavior, Jacob's relationship with his Uncle Laban became very hostile, and Jacob fled with his wives and all his possessions to head back to his homeland (Gen. 29:25; 30:25-36). However, when Laban found out what had happened, he followed after Jacob and overtook him with intention to harm him.

> **READ GENESIS 31:24,29.** How did God protect Jacob and his family from Laban?

After his encounter with Laban, Jacob walked into another tumultuous situation. The conflict with his brother Esau (the one he stole the blessing and birthright from!) had not been settled. So on his way home, messengers came and told Jacob that his brother Esau was coming to meet him and he had four hundred men with him. Needless to say, Jacob was afraid of what Esau and his men would do to him and his family.

What is the first thing Jacob did upon hearing this news (Gen. 32:9-12)?

Whose words did he repeat while doing this (v. 9)? Why is this significant? Look up Genesis 28:13; 31:3 to help you with your answer.

How did Esau's response to Jacob in Genesis 33:4 illustrate God's protection of Jacob and his family?

In his prayer to God, Jacob repeated the promises that God had given him (Gen. 32:9). No matter what happened, God had promised to help His chosen people, Abraham's descendants, to overcome. So, through the harrowing incidents Jacob and his family experienced, God remained committed to protecting the promise.

READ GENESIS 37:1-11.

Where were Jacob and his family living?

What do we learn about his son, Joseph? What do we learn about his relationship with Jacob and his brothers? Why do you think these details are included?

In the following chart, summarize Joseph's two dreams (Gen. 37:5-10).

Dream One	Dream Two

How did Joseph's brothers and father react to his dreams? Why did they react this way?

Joseph's brothers were already not fond of their younger brother, so hearing about his dreams didn't warm their affections for him. The impact of their jealousy reached a climax when they ended up selling their brother into slavery and then faking his death so Jacob wouldn't know what really happened to his favorite son. Talk about a complicated family dynamic!

After being sold to Midianite traders, Joseph ended up in Egypt as a slave to Potiphar, an officer of Pharaoh. He found favor with Potiphar, becoming his personal attendant, and had charge of Potiphar's entire household and all that he owned. Life was going well for Joseph until Potiphar's wife falsely accused him of rape, which resulted in Potiphar sending Joseph to prison. But while in prison, Joseph found favor with the prison warden, who gave him leadership of all the prisoners.

COMPARE GENESIS 39:2 WITH VERSES 21 AND 23. What repeated phrase is found in each of these verses? Why do you think it is repeated?

Despite the difficult things Joseph experienced, the Lord was with him, working out His plan for Joseph and His people. Eventually, Joseph was released from prison and put in leadership as second in command under Pharaoh. During his time of leadership, the land of Egypt experienced a great famine. Because Joseph had led the nation to stockpile grain in the years prior to the famine, everyone had to come to see Joseph in order to get food, including Joseph's father and brothers. But when they came to request provisions from the leadership in Egypt, they were unaware that the person they were asking for help was the brother they had previously sold into slavery.

In Genesis 45, Joseph revealed his identity to his brothers.

> According to him, what was the divine purpose of their malicious actions (Gen. 45:7-8)? Read Genesis 50:20 to help with your answer.

> Can you look back on hurtful events or difficult seasons in your past and see now how God was working? If so, explain.

Over several years and through unexpected circumstances, God worked through Joseph to provide for his entire family. God upheld the covenant He made with Abraham. Showering Abraham's descendants with grace, He protected them despite "barrenness, sin, stupidity, squabbles, and famine."[3] Even though their offspring were not yet as numerous as the sand on the seashore, Joseph, his brothers, and their families were blessed.

> At the end of Genesis, where were the descendants of Abraham living?

> Why is this significant?

The opening pages of Exodus tell us that after Joseph and his brothers died, "the Israelites [the descendants of Jacob's sons] were fruitful, increased rapidly, multiplied, and became extremely numerous so that the land was filled with them" (Ex. 1:7). But after a long season of prosperity and peace, another threat to the promises of God arose in the land of Egypt. A new king came to power "who did not know about Joseph" (v. 8). When he noticed how numerous and powerful the Israelites had become, he enslaved them. But still, the Israelites multiplied. So the king of Egypt commanded the Israelite midwives to let the newborn daughters live but kill all the baby boys. However, because these midwives feared God more than the king, they disobeyed his commands, and the people of God continued to thrive. Pharaoh then instructed his people to throw every Hebrew baby boy into the Nile.

One such baby boy was not thrown into the Nile but strategically placed there by his mother so that he might have a chance at life. When Pharaoh's daughter came to bathe in the Nile, she found the Hebrew baby and took him to be her son. She named him Moses (Ex. 2:1-10).

Moses grew up in Pharaoh's household intimately aware of the suffering of his people. Witnessing an Egyptian beating a Hebrew, he responded in vengeance by killing the Egyptian. This decision resulted in Moses having to flee for his life. But even though he was hiding from Pharaoh and the Egyptians as a shepherd in the fields of Midian, Moses could not hide from God.

READ EXODUS 3:1-13.

What caught Moses's attention while tending his father-in-law's flock (vv. 2-3)?

What name did God use to identify Himself to Moses (v. 6)?

Describe the assignment God asked Moses to fulfill. What was the motivation for God's request (vv. 7-10)

How did Moses respond (vv. 11-13)? Is this how you would have expected him to respond? Explain.

The stories of Abraham, Isaac, Jacob, and Joseph teach us how God works through unexpected people to accomplish His plans. He doesn't choose people because they meet some standard of morality or excellence, but rather in His sovereignty, God chooses whomever He wants. We will see the same to be true with Moses. God asked him to step into a significant leadership role that required courage and fortitude. But Moses lacked both of those qualities. He was a man living in hiding, fearful of taking on the divine mission he was given.

Rather than start over with someone else, God provided Moses with the support he needed. With the help of his brother Aaron and the God-given power to do miracles, Moses returned to Egypt to lead his people out of slavery and into the promised land. Several times Moses met with Pharaoh to try to convince him to set the Hebrew people free. But each time Moses was met with opposition.

READ EXODUS 7:3-5.

Why did Moses have difficulty convincing Pharaoh to let the Hebrew people go free?

How did God plan on responding to Pharaoh's hardened heart? What was He going to accomplish by doing this?

Through Moses, God responded to Pharaoh's opposition by sending a total of ten plagues. These plagues were designed to execute judgment against Egypt and their gods, showing God's sovereign power and supremacy. With each new plague, the judgment of God grew worse and worse leading up to the final plague—the death of every firstborn male in Egypt (Ex. 11). After the death of his firstborn son, Pharaoh finally relented and allowed all of Israel to leave Egypt. But as we will see tomorrow, his change of heart did not last for long.

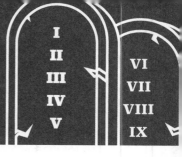

Day 4

OUT OF EGYPT

After four hundred years, God answered the Israelites' cries and sent Moses to help deliver them out of slavery. God had promised Israel a life of blessing and physical fruitfulness in the land of Canaan. While it seemed as if the unrelenting anger of Pharaoh was blocking the fulfillment of this promise, today we will learn how God used Pharaoh to launch Israel into her next season.

After the devastating tenth plague, Pharaoh told Moses and the people to get out immediately (Ex. 12:31-32). So they did. But later, Pharaoh regretted his decision. He gathered his troops and pursued the Israelites, catching up to them at the edge of the Red Sea.

> What did the Israelites say when they saw the Egyptians coming after them (Ex. 14:10-12)?

> How did Moses respond to them? Rewrite Exodus 14:13-14 in your own words.

After reminding Israel of her guaranteed deliverance by the power of God, Moses lifted his staff, and God parted the Red Sea (Ex. 14:21). Then Moses guided Israel across on dry land. The Egyptian army followed them. But as soon as all of Israel crossed over, God, through Moses, closed the water back over the Egyptian army; none of them survived.

The people of Israel were now free and walking toward the land of promise. But on their way there, they stopped to meet with God at Mount Sinai. There, God made another covenant with Israel through Moses. Through this covenant, God gave instructions on how to live as His people—loving Him and loving each other.

READ EXODUS 19:5-6. In this passage, God used two key phrases to describe Israel. Write out each phrase by filling in the blanks below. I'm using the CSB translation.

"Now if you will carefully listen to me and keep my covenant, you will be my own possession out of all the peoples, although the whole earth is mine, and you will be my kingdom of (1) _____ and my (2) _____ nation." These are the words that you are to say to the Israelites.

Look up the words you wrote for blanks one and two in a dictionary and write a definition for them below.

(1) _____:

(2) _____:

God's constant objective was to establish His kingdom on earth, and the law was given to not only define a standard of morality but also form a community.[4] In His kingdom, humanity was designed to live as vice-regents, or sub-rulers, stewarding God's kingdom in such a way that everything and everyone would thrive. The law God gave Israel was designed to show Israel how to live out this divine design.

While they were at Mount Sinai, God called Moses up on the mountain to give him the content of the law. God gave Moses many different instructions for how Israel was supposed to live in relationship with Him and with each other. While the law consists of several hundred rules, the part that many of us are most familiar with is the Ten Commandments.

READ EXODUS 20:1-17. What important reminder did God give Israel in verse 2? Explain why.

What is the main focus of each group of commandments?
Match each group with the correct answer.

Commandments 1–4   a. Israel's relationship with others
Commandments 5–10   b. Israel's relationship with God
                                         c. Israel's relationship with nature
                                         d. Israel's relationship with each other

Write out the first commandment below. How would keeping this commandment help Israel keep every other commandment?

By keeping the law, Israel would be able to honor the covenant made with God. This covenant established the terms of the Israelites' relationship with God and helped them live out their divine design as image bearers in God's kingdom community. It instructed and guided the people in their spread of justice and *shalom* as they loved God and loved others.[5]

In addition to the Ten Commandments, God told the people of Israel what would happen if they obeyed the law—God would bless them greatly—and what would happen if they disobeyed the law—God would hold them accountable through a series of harsh consequences. In Exodus 23:20-33, God gave a series of promises and warnings, many of which we will see the Israelites experience during their time in the promised land.

One major focus of these promises and warnings was the Israelites' relationship with the other people around them. Why did Israel need to drive out the nations that were in the land of Canaan? What would happen if Israel didn't (vv. 23-24,31-33)?

After Israel committed to do all that God had told her, God gave Moses instructions on how to build a tabernacle for Him. Remember, the definition of God's kingdom is God's people in God's place under God's rule and blessing.[6] As reflected through the Mosaic Covenant, God chose Israel to be His people and had established the terms of His rule and blessing. The tabernacle would be God's place, where He would dwell among His people in the sanctuary (Ex. 25:8; 29:45-46).

In Leviticus, God gave the people of Israel instructions for how they should worship Him in the tabernacle. These instructions included the sacrifices the Israelites would have to make whenever they sinned. Even though they had the law, sin still existed, and God would make provision for the Israelites to be cleansed from their sin through the process of atonement. To echo the words of Patrick Schreiner, "to enter the presence of God, to be the people of God, to be in the place of God, to be the kingdom of priests and the holy nation, the sins of the people had to be dealt with."[7] Sacrifice was the means through which the relationship between a holy God and Israel was maintained. But Israel's sacrifices were ultimately insufficient because they only provided a temporary covering for sin. Each new year brought with it a renewed requirement for atonement. The people of Israel needed a permanent sacrifice; they needed a Savior.

The book of Numbers details Israel's journey through the wilderness to the promised land. For forty years, Moses led the Israelites, navigating their seasons of obedience and disobedience with God. But by God's grace, they finally made it to the shores of the Jordan River, a body of water on whose opposite shore was the promised land of Canaan.

Lastly, in Deuteronomy, Moses shared his final words with the Israelites before they crossed over into the promised land. Before he died, He detailed their journey through the wilderness, the law God gave them, and the promises and warnings attached to their obedience and/or disobedience to the law.

> According to Moses, how was Israel's experience in the promised land going to be connected to her obedience to the covenant (Deut. 6:1-3)?

> What repeated instruction did Moses give in Deuteronomy 6:18-19; 7:1-6? What would happen if Israel did not obey it (Deut. 28:15,63-64)?

Each year, Israel observed the Day of Atonement—an annual ceremony when the nation would be cleansed from sin. The ceremony included the high priest sacrificing a male goat as a purification offering, satisfying the wrath of God. Then the high priest would lay his hands on a second goat (scapegoat) and confess over it all of Israel's sins. The goat was then sent off into the wilderness, removing the sin and guilt from Israel (Lev. 16).

Moses ended Deuteronomy by recounting all the blessings Israel would experience if the Israelites obeyed God's rule and all the harsh consequences they would experience if they disobeyed. Many of the promises God made to Abraham were about to be fulfilled. But as Israel took hold of the land of promise, two questions lingered—*Would the Israelites be faithful to the covenant, or would they be disobedient and get exiled from the land?*[8] *And would God keep His promise, remaining faithful, even if the Israelites were unfaithful?*

Stay tuned.

Day 5

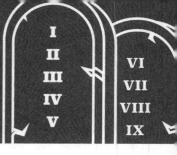

WEEKLY REVIEW

This week we walked through our third session of the grand narrative of Scripture when God made covenant promises with Abraham, Moses, and Israel to restore His kingdom. Answer the questions below to summarize this week's main points. Feel free to use bullet points.

1. What is a covenant?

2. What three promises were included in the covenant God made with Abraham?

3. What happened to Israel (Abraham's descendants) in Egypt, and how did God use Moses to help them?

4. What did God give Moses and Israel as a sign of His covenant with them?

5. What would happen to Israel if the Israelites remained faithful to the covenant they made with God? What consequences would they experience if they acted unfaithfully?

6. How was Israel able to remain holy in the presence of a holy God?

SUMMARIZE THE NARRATIVE

In the space below, use your answers to the previous questions to create a two to three sentence summary of what happened this session in the grand narrative of Scripture.

Video + Group Guide

SESSION THREE

WATCH Session Three video teaching and take notes below.

To access the video teaching sessions, use the instructions in the back of your Bible study book.

DISCUSSION QUESTIONS

1   How would you explain *covenant* to someone?

2   What was significant about the covenant God made with Abraham?

3   How do you see God accomplishing His purpose through the stories we heard today?

4   What was the purpose of the Mosaic covenant? What implications does it have for us today?

5   What does it mean that we are to be holy as God is holy? How are you living that out?

6   What is one point or truth that really stood out to you from the video teaching? Why?

THE STATUS OF THE KINGDOM

In the chart below, fill in the blanks to review the definition of the kingdom of God. (Look back at your notes on p. 13 if you need help). At the close of each teaching video, I will update the status of each phrase.

The Kingdom of God	A Promise to Restore the Kingdom
God's _____ in	
God's _____ under	
God's _____ and _____.	

SESSION FOUR

A Divided Kingdom

Timeline
SESSION FOUR

* The second king of Israel was David, who in many ways became Israel's greatest king, but even greater, God chose David's line to bring forth the true King, Jesus.

JOSHUA LEADS THE ISRAELITES INTO THE PROMISED LAND

**KINGS
Saul, David, and Solomon**

1200 BC   1100 BC   1000 BC   900 BC

TIME OF THE JUDGES

DIVIDED KINGDOM

BOOKS

JOSHUA

JUDGES

RUTH

1 KINGS

2 KINGS

1 CHRONICLES

2 CHRONICLES

EZRA

NEHEMIAH

ESTHER

* The "judges" in the book of Judges were not courtroom figures but more like political, tribal, military leaders.[1]

MEMORABLE WORDS
That whole generation was also gathered to their ancestors. After them another generation rose up who did not know the LORD or the works he had done for Israel.
Judges 2:10

* After the time of the judges, the people of Israel came to Samuel and asked for a king "like all the other nations" (1 Sam. 8:20). Although their motive was wrong, God agreed to give them a king. Saul became the first king of Israel.

Haven't I commanded you: be strong and courageous? Do not be afraid or discouraged, for the LORD your God is with you wherever you go.

Joshua 1:9

* 538 BC
King Cyrus of Persia declares that the Jewish captives can return to their homeland.

DISOBEDIENCE AND EXILE

FUN FACT

The oldest existing monarchy in the world is the Imperial House of Japan, which was founded in 660 BC.[2]

CAPTIVES RETURN

800 BC   700 BC   600 BC   500 BC

* 722 BC
The Northern Kingdom of Israel falls to the Assyrians. The people are taken off into exile.

* 586 BC
The Southern Kingdom falls to the Babylonians. The people are taken off into exile.

* ELIJAH the prophet served the Lord in the Northern Kingdom of Israel during the reigns of Ahab and Ahaziah. He did not die but was taken to heaven in a chariot of fire (2 Kings 2:9-12).

* ELISHA the prophet was a disciple of Elijah. He was present when Elijah was taken into heaven and took up the prophetic mantle at that time.

Day 1

JOSHUA AND JUDGES

Last week, we left Israel on the banks of the Jordan River waiting to cross over into the promised land. Before he died, Moses reminded the Israelites of their commitment to live in covenantal relationship with God. Through Israel, God was working to rebuild His kingdom and bring blessing to the entire world. With them numbering about two million people at this time, God had made Abraham's descendants as numerous as the stars in the sky and had brought them to the promised land of Canaan. This would be the place where God would rule over His people while using them to bless the entire world. But as the people of Israel entered the land, they would be tempted to worship other gods rather than worship the one true God. As we make our trek from Joshua through Esther, we will see whether the Israelites chose to be faithful to God and live in the land or if they disobeyed and were exiled from the land.

Note: This week our pace will start to speed up as we will walk through several books of the Bible each day! Remember, the goal of our journey is not to cover every detail of the narrative of Scripture but to highlight the details that make the sixty-six books of the Bible one unified story.

Let's jump in!

> **READ JOSHUA 1:1-9.** What phrase did God repeat to Joshua? Why do you think He did this?

God assured Joshua that He would be with him as Joshua led the people. He exhorted Joshua to be strong and courageous, and as long as Joshua was obedient to the Word of God, he would be successful.

Like Moses, Joshua led Israel to live in obedience to the Lord. For this reason, we see God grant continual favor to Israel. Many times this favor was manifested through victory in battle. In total, Joshua and Israel fought over thirty kings to take hold of the land God promised them. Joshua then split up the land among the twelve tribes of Israel as an inheritance, and they spent several years peacefully living in the land.

Right before he died, Joshua gave Israel two different "farewell" messages. Similar to the words of Moses in Deuteronomy, Joshua reminded the people of God's faithfulness. Recounting the story of God's blessing in Canaan and the entirety of their journey from Egypt, Joshua challenged Israel to stay committed to God as both their Lord and their King.

READ JOSHUA 23:6-8.

List Joshua's instructions to the nation of Israel.

What would happen if Israel did not heed Joshua's instructions (Josh. 23:16)?

By the end of the book of Joshua, which of these three promises God made to Abraham had been fulfilled?

_____ Abraham's descendants were as numerous as the stars of the sky.

_____ Abraham's descendants lived in Canaan.

_____ Abraham's descendants were providing blessing to all the people on earth.

At this point in the story, many of God's promises to Abraham had been fulfilled, including the promise of people and blessing. But the full realization of God's promise of blessing was yet to come. After the death of Joshua, Israel continued to drive out the nations that were still in the land of Canaan. By the hand of God, several of the tribes of Israel were able to conquer the foreign nations around them. But many of the tribes were unsuccessful due to their disobedience to God (Judg. 1:21–3:5).

How did God respond to their disobedience (Judg. 2:1-3)?

After Joshua's death and the death of his contemporaries, the author of Judges wrote these chilling words:

> And all that generation also were gathered to their fathers. And there arose another generation after them who did not know the LORD or the work that he had done for Israel. And the people of Israel did what was evil in the sight of the LORD and served the Baals.
>
> JUDGES 2:10-11 (ESV)

The people of Israel abandoned the Lord, and He responded to their disobedience by handing them over to their enemies. The people fell into a devastating cycle of behavior.

READ JUDGES 2:16-23 and summarize their cycle of behavior.

How did Israel compromise in Judges 3:6? How does this connect with the warning Joshua gave Israel in Joshua 23:6-8?

What are some of the "false gods" or "false stories" (refer to "A Word from the Author" on pp. 8–9) the world tempts us to worship or believe in? Why is it important that we be aware of this as we lovingly engage the culture and our unbelieving neighbors?

Rather than stay faithful to the covenant they made with God, the Israelites started to worship the gods of the nations they failed to drive out of Canaan.

One phrase that the biblical authors used to describe their behavior is "they prostituted themselves." In future stories, we will also hear Israel referred to as adulterous (Jer. 3:8; Hos. 2:2). These descriptors are meant to be as shocking as they sound. The biblical authors used marriage as a metaphor to explain the depth of Israel's relationship with God. Israel had joined in a covenantal relationship with God, but instead of being faithful to Him, the Israelites "cheated" on Him with other gods.

The story of Judges is the story of the Israelites' unfaithfulness to God. Instead of worshiping Him as their Lord and King, they worshiped the gods of the nations around them. But even though they were unfaithful to the covenant, God was not. In response to their sin, God faithfully used Israel's enemies to punish Israel. But after years of oppression, the Israelites cried out to God for deliverance. He then raised up a judge to help save them. They would live peaceably for a while until their cycle of unfaithfulness started over again. While there are a few bright moments during this part of Israel's history, for most of the time Israel continued to spiral down into chaos.

> According to the author of Judges, what was causing Israel's
> problematic behavior (Judg. 21:25)? Look up Deuteronomy 17:14-20
> to help with your answer.

The judges that God raised up were a sign of His love and faithfulness to Israel. But the nation needed a better solution; they needed a leader who would help Israel bring blessing to the entire world. Israel needed a leader that would point the Israelites in the way of righteousness, away from their path of sin. Israel needed a king, the one Moses spoke about in Deuteronomy. This king would help Israel live out her divine identity and purpose as a sub-ruler in God's kingdom. He would rule the Israelites in such a way that they flourished and were able to help everyone and everything around them do the same. This king would be the means through which God mediates His kingdom on earth!

But at the end of Judges, we are left wondering what king Israel would choose. *Would the Israelites choose a king like the nations or a king that God chose?*

We'll find out tomorrow!

Day 2

DESIRE FOR A KING

The book of Ruth is probably one of the most misunderstood books in Scripture. Many of us might be familiar with its contents because it was taught to us as a guide for marriage. As a single woman, I can't count how many times I've been told to "go and get my Boaz." While I won't deny the beauty of the story between Ruth and Boaz, the biblical author's focus wasn't on romance and marriage. Rather he was using Ruth's story to point us toward the theme of kingship. And this shouldn't be a surprise, right? We just finished hearing how badly Israel needed the right king! The book of Ruth will give us hope that a king was on the way.

READ RUTH 1:1-5. Use the chart to summarize what you learn.

During what time period did this story occur?	
Who was Naomi?	
Who was Ruth?	

Following the tragic events recorded in verses 1-5, Naomi, Ruth, and Orpah headed back to Bethlehem. Along the way, Naomi insisted that both young women return to their homes. While Orpah did turn back, Ruth confessed her love and commitment to Naomi and her desire to continue on the journey. They arrived in Bethlehem right before the barley harvest. In God's grace, Ruth found work gleaning the fields of a man named Boaz. This opportunity provided food for her and her mother-in-law and also turned into an opportunity for marriage.

Boaz was Ruth's kinsman-redeemer, a close relative that was supposed to marry her because her first husband died. In a beautiful turn of events, Ruth went from being destitute to being Boaz's wife. But what is even more interesting about her story is to whom she gave birth. Unbeknownst to her, Ruth's son would be the grandfather of Israel's king (Ruth 4:13-22)!

READ RUTH 4:13-22. List the name of Ruth's son, grandson, and great-grandson.

In the first few chapters of 1 Samuel, we read about the birth and ministry of Israel's last judge, Samuel. After faithfully leading Israel for many, many years, Samuel appointed his sons to take his place. But his sons were sinful and disobedient (1 Sam. 8:3). So the elders of Israel came to Samuel and demanded he appoint a king to rule them.

READ 1 SAMUEL 8:4-9. What kind of king did Israel want?

What about this request was dishonoring to God? (Look back to Deut. 17:14-15.) How did Samuel and God respond to Israel's request?

The problem with the Israelites' request wasn't that they wanted a king; it was that they wanted a king like the nations. Rather than have a king under God, they wanted a king instead of God. Their request to be like the other nations was actually a rejection of God's kingship and rule over them.[2] But in His grace, God gave the Israelites what they wanted.

READ 1 SAMUEL 8:10-22. What does this passage tell us about how Israel's desired king would treat them?

The kinsman-redeemer was usually a blood relative who faced certain obligations under the law of levirate marriage. If his brother died an untimely death without having a son, the kinsman-redeemer was to marry his brother's wife and raise up a male descendant to carry on the family name.[1]

How did Israel respond to Samuel's warning? What reasons did they give for wanting a king (v. 20)?

What's something you've asked God for with the wrong motive? How did that turn out for you?

God, in His grace, gave the Israelites what they wanted and anointed Saul as king. But rather than bringing blessing to Israel, Saul proved to be a king who followed after his own way rather than the way of God. We see this specifically on two different occasions. First, in 1 Samuel 13, Saul grew impatient waiting for Samuel to come and conduct the sacrifice before a battle with the Philistines. So, he performed the sacrifice himself. Then in 1 Samuel 15, Samuel gave Saul clear instructions to destroy the enemy completely (v. 3). But instead of being obedient, Saul and his troops kept all of the best plunder for themselves.

How did God, through Samuel, respond to Saul's disobedience (1 Sam. 13:13-14; 15:26-28)?

After Saul's kingship was taken from him, the story quickly pivots to focus on his replacement—David. He was the youngest of eight sons and from the small town of Bethlehem. He quickly confirmed his kingship by the way he led Israel in battle against the Philistines. While Saul cowered in fear, David boldly defended the name of God and the people of Israel (1 Sam. 17). But instead of accepting David as king, Saul sought to kill him. David spent several years running from Saul, waiting patiently to take the throne and rule over Israel.

READ 2 SAMUEL 5:1-2. In your own words, summarize the way God said David would lead Israel.

When David had settled into his kingship, living in peace in his kingdom, he decided he wanted to build a home for the Lord. Remember the tabernacle we talked about last week? At this point in Israel's history, the place of God's dwelling was in a tent. But David wanted to build God a permanent structure. Through the prophet Nathan, God responded to David's request, telling him that his son would build Him a house. Yet God also made a covenant with David, reaffirming His commitment to Israel and His plan of restoration.

> **READ 2 SAMUEL 7:8-16** and summarize the covenantal promises God made with David. (Hint: All the promises usually start with or include the phrase "I will.")
>
> Promise One (v. 9)
>
> Promise Two (v. 10)
>
> Promise Three (v. 11)
>
> Promise Four (vv. 12-13,16)

In the Davidic Covenant, God built on the covenants He made with both Abraham and Moses. He reaffirmed the promises He had already made and then promised that David's kingdom, or rule, would last forever. Out of the land God had given Israel would come a leader from the line of David through whom blessing would flow to the entire world. The promised king would be someone far greater than David, ruling Israel perfectly for the glory of God. Eventually, we will see that great David's greater Son will be the Lord Jesus Christ (Luke 11:31)![3]

The rest of 2 Samuel details the reign of David. While he led Israel to worship God, David also committed several grievous acts of sin. As king of Israel, he used his power in ways that caused death, both in the family of his victim and his own family. David would turn back to the Lord but experienced the consequences of his sin for the rest of his life. Even though Israel lived in peace and prosperity under David's reign, his shortcomings highlighted the need for a better king: God's King.

And while Israel would have many kings after David, Israel would wait a long time for the one true King to arrive.

Day 3

THE KINGDOM'S DOWNFALL

There were times in Scripture when Israel experienced long periods of prosperity and victory. These were the seasons in which the people's king guided them to live in obedience to the law, the covenant they made with God through Moses. First Kings 1–11 tells us about one such season, specifically the time during which Israel was led by King Solomon.

After his father died and the kingdom was established in his hands (1 Kings 2:46), Solomon began his reign by offering a thousand burnt offerings on the altar at Gibeon. At this time of sacrifice, Solomon had an experience with the Lord that would completely change the trajectory of his leadership, giving him an indispensable skill that would bring blessing to all of Israel.

READ 1 KINGS 3:7-14.

How many times did Solomon use the word *your/yours*?

Explain the significance of Solomon's view of himself and Israel in these verses.

Look up the word *discern* in a dictionary and write the definition in your own words. Then look up the word in a thesaurus and add a few synonyms that fit the way the word is used in verse 9.

discern	

What did Solomon not ask for that pleased God (vv. 10-11)?

What three things did God give Solomon? What did Solomon have to do to receive the last gift?

Solomon's rule brought prosperity and peace to Israel. His leadership was characterized by an unmatched level of wisdom, so much so that people from around the world came to learn from him. Much of this wisdom is captured for us in the three books of the Bible that Solomon authored: Proverbs, Ecclesiastes, and Song of Songs. In these books, "wisdom" is all about knowing how to live God's way in God's world, glorifying Him in a good but fallen world. Proverbs 1:7 tells us that wisdom begins with "the fear of the LORD"—that is, a heartfelt reverence for the Lord as the Creator and Redeemer.[4] Solomon's leadership was a prime example of this, as we see how his dependence upon God resulted in an overflow of blessing. But the pinnacle of Solomon's leadership over Israel would be the completion of the temple he built for God. This structure would be built out of the finest materials available to Solomon at that time (1 Kings 6:14-38). He would spare no expense to build a structure worthy of the Lord.

In 1 Kings 8:14-21, Solomon gave a speech during the temple dedication and recounted the promises that God made to his father, David. How had God fulfilled His promise to David?

Through Solomon's leadership, how had God fulfilled His promises of land, people, and blessing to Abraham and Moses (1 Kings 8:54-56)? Use the chart below to give your best answer.

How many people were a part of Israel (1 Kings 4:20)?	
What land did Israel occupy (1 Kings 4:21)?	
Were the people of Israel living under the rule and blessing of God? Were they being a blessing to the nations around them? Explain (1 Kings 8:1-11; 10:1-13).	

The completion of the temple was a significant moment in the life of Israel. Evidenced by the cloud of glory that filled the temple, God, who led Israel throughout the wilderness, now dwelt with His people in Jerusalem. This city would become Israel's capital city and the place where the people would go to meet with God. This moment of peace and prosperity could make it seem as though what was broken in Eden has finally been restored. God was dwelling with His people as they submitted to His rule through the leadership of King Solomon. This moment of *shalom* brought blessing to Israel and presented an opportunity for Israel to be a blessing to the nations.

But after the dedication, God warned Solomon that Israel's blessing and His presence among the people required that they be faithful to the covenant they made with Him (1 Kings 9:1-9). While it seemed as if Solomon and the people would obey, 1 Kings 11 tells us otherwise.

READ 1 KINGS 11:1-4.

What warning from God did Solomon not heed?

How did Solomon's disobedience lead to spiritual compromise?

READ VERSES 11-13. How did God respond to Solomon's actions? Use the chart below to describe the impact of Solomon's decision.

How would Solomon's actions impact him?	
How would Solomon's actions impact Solomon's son?	

After Solomon died, his son Rehoboam took the throne. The ten northern and eastern tribes of Israel rose up against him and established their own kingdom under Jeroboam.[5] The kingdom that experienced 120 years of unity under the leadership of Saul, David, and Solomon quickly declined because of division and idolatry. The Northern Kingdom (ten tribes) was called Israel, and the Southern Kingdom (two tribes) was called Judah. Although the Southern Kingdom had a few good kings sprinkled in among the monarchy, collectively Israel and Judah's kings were an epic failure, leading them to worship the idols of the nations around them.

God was patient with Israel and sent prophets to remind the people of the covenant they made with Him. For a long time, God worked through these men to draw Israel back into a place of obedience. After about two hundred years of disobedience and idolatry, God honored the covenant He made with Israel. But this time, what He gave them was not blessing but judgment.

READ 2 KINGS 17:6-7 AND 2 KINGS 24:10-17. Use the chart below to summarize what happened to the Northern Kingdom (Israel) and Southern Kingdom (Judah). (Hint: The capital of the Northern Kingdom was Samaria.)

	Northern Kingdom (Israel) 2 Kings 17:6-7	Southern Kingdom (Judah) 2 Kings 24:10-17
Who attacked them?		
Where were the exiles taken?		
Who was taken, and who was left behind? (If these details are given.)		

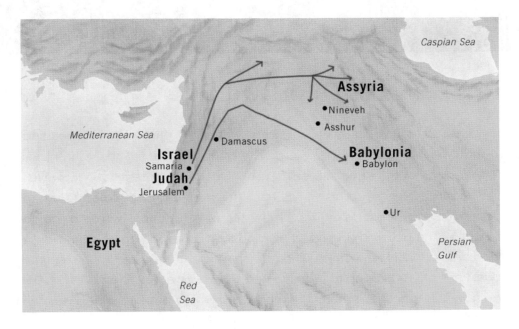

Both the Northern and Southern Kingdoms were taken into exile, respectively in 722 BC and 586 BC. Remember the importance of the temple in Jerusalem? When Babylon captured the Southern Kingdom, the Babylonians set fire to the king's palace and the temple. The Israelites' beloved city of Jerusalem was reduced to ruins, and most of Judah was marched off to Babylon as slaves. To say that Israel's (both the Northern and Southern Kingdoms) situation seemed hopeless would be an understatement. Israel went from thriving under the leadership of Solomon to living as exiles in Babylon and Assyria. No longer were the Israelites under the blessing of God, and they sure weren't providing blessing to the nations.

But even though God was not dwelling with His people, He had not forgotten them. In the same way that He sent prophets to warn Israel, He would send prophets to give them hope. God would deliver His people, and one day their exile would end.

Day 4

RETURN AND REBUILD

If you read through 1 and 2 Chronicles, you might think you are rereading 1 and 2 Samuel and 1 and 2 Kings. The reason is that 1 and 2 Chronicles repeat some of the same stories that are covered in those books. However, the chronicler recorded his words after the people of Israel had returned from exile and (spoiler alert) rebuilt the temple. But things were not going as well as the people had hoped, leaving them questioning whether or not God would fulfill His promises. So, the chronicler attempted to answer the questions of God's people: *Who are we? How did we get here? What do we do now?* Despite the exile, the author was showing Israel that God was still in control, and He would be faithful to restore.[6]

SKIM THROUGH 1 CHRONICLES 1–9.

Who was the first name mentioned in the genealogies (1 Chron. 1:1)?

The twelve tribes had their roots in Jacob's twelve sons. Rank the amount of space given to each son's descendants from least to greatest. (1 is the least; 12 is the greatest.) (Hint: The tribes of Ephraim and Manasseh find their roots in Joseph's family line.)

1.

2.

3.

4.

5.

6.

7.

8.

9.

10.

11.

12.

The chronicler retold the story of Israel with an intentional focus on the line of David, reminding Israel that the promises God made to David were not nullified and would still be fulfilled.[7] His highlighting of David was also manifested through the stories about David and Solomon he did not cover and the new ones he included. The chronicler was not omitting those details to ignore David's faults but rather focusing on David's strengths and godliness to give hope to the nation. The covenant with David promised that a future King was coming who would be better than David and Solomon.[8] And, with the chronicler's focus on the temple, he was also reminding Israel of the centrality of worship. The temple was where God dwelt with His people, and worship reminded Israel that He was their King and Lord.

> **READ 2 CHRONICLES 36:21-23.** How did the chronicler end his book? Why is it significant he did not end the story at verse 21?

The book of Ezra picks up where 2 Chronicles ends, detailing the proclamation of King Cyrus. After years and years of exile, the people of Israel were about to see God fulfill His promises of blessing and restoration.

READ EZRA 1:1-4. How does this passage connect with the final words of 2 Chronicles? Use the chart below to summarize your answer.

What was King Cyrus sending Israel to do?	
Where was he sending the Israelites to do it?	
How would this task be funded?	

The book of Ezra recounts Israel's return from exile and the people's efforts to rebuild the temple. The original group of returnees, led by a man named Zerubbabel, worked for a time to rebuild the temple, but because of opposition, the project stalled. Years later, Ezra led a new group of people back to Jerusalem, and they finished what the first group started. But upon his return, Ezra found that opposition to the building of the temple was not the only problem Israel had.

READ EZRA 9:1-3. Summarize what the leaders told Ezra about the people. How did Ezra respond to the news? Explain why.

Even though the people had returned from exile, they had fallen into the same disobedient behavioral patterns that led them into exile. This same dynamic is also present in the book of Nehemiah. Similar to Ezra, Nehemiah led a group of returnees back to Jerusalem from Babylon. Instead of working on the temple, Nehemiah led the people to rebuild the walls of Jerusalem. Like Ezra, he experienced opposition to his project, and he also saw how the people were being unfaithful to the covenant (Neh. 5:1-11).

How did Nehemiah (Ezra and the Levites) try to correct the behavior of the people (Neh. 8:1-3,9-12; 9:1-3)?

In what way does the ending of Nehemiah show us the result of their attempts to draw Israel back into covenant faithfulness with the Lord (Neh. 13:23-27)?

Israel returned from exile and successfully rebuilt the temple and the walls of Jerusalem under the leadership of Ezra and Nehemiah. Yet even with the restoration of their city's infrastructure, Israel still had the same problem that led her into exile—sin.

No matter how hard the Israelites tried, they consistently chose to worship foreign gods, intermarry with the other nations, and mistreat each other. Ezra and Nehemiah reminded them of the law, and the people of Israel recommitted to follow it. However, they soon fell back into their sinful patterns.

So, what do Ezra and Nehemiah show us then? Israel needed the promised Messiah. Though God was faithful to the promise to bring Israel back to Jerusalem, the Israelites remained in spiritual exile from His presence. They were being reminded that deliverance was coming.

The book of Esther follows the books of Ezra and Nehemiah. But, chronologically, the events this book describes took place in the middle of the Ezra-Nehemiah story, between chapters 6–7 of Ezra.[9] One of the most interesting facts about the book of Esther is that it does not mention God's name specifically.[10] However, He is present throughout the book as it details how God alone preserved the Jewish people from being annihilated.[11] Written after the return from exile, the book of Esther reminded Israel that nothing would thwart God's plan to fulfill His covenant with Abraham and bring blessing to Israel. The promised Messianic King was coming!

Day 5

WEEKLY REVIEW

This week we walked through our fourth session of the grand narrative of Scripture—the history of Israel's monarchy. Answer the questions below to summarize this week's main points. Feel free to use bullet points.

1. What major task did Israel complete under Joshua's leadership?

2. After Joshua, and those who led with him, died, how did God respond to the Israelites' covenant unfaithfulness? Did this help them stop worshiping foreign gods? Why or why not?

3. Why did Israel ask for a king? What was the difference between Israel's first two kings?

4. What new promise did God make in His covenant with David?

5. After Solomon built the temple, did he lead the people of Israel to be faithful to their covenant with God? How did his actions affect the rest of Israel's kings?

6. What important events occurred in 722 BC and 586 BC? What was significant about these events?

SUMMARIZE THE NARRATIVE

In the space below, use your answers to the previous questions to create a two to three sentence summary of what happened this session in the grand narrative of Scripture.

Video + Group Guide

SESSION FOUR

WATCH Session Four video teaching and take notes below.

To access the video teaching sessions, use the instructions in the back of your Bible study book.

DISCUSSION QUESTIONS

1   How did God show His faithfulness to the Israelites?

2   While God remained faithful to them, did they stay devoted to Him? What happened? Do you see yourself in their story? Explain.

3   What was the purpose of God's judgment on the Israelites?

4   Why did the people want a king? Were they wrong in their request? Explain.

5   What can we learn from this era of God's people?

6   What is one point or truth that really stood out to you from the video teaching? Why?

THE STATUS OF THE KINGDOM

In the chart below, fill in the blanks to review the definition of the kingdom of God. (Look back at your notes on p. 13 if you need help). At the close of each teaching video, I will update the status of each phrase.

The Kingdom of God	A Divided Kingdom
God's _____ in	
God's _____ under	
God's _____ and _____.	

SESSION FIVE

Life in the Kingdom

Timeline

SESSION FIVE

This week's time line shows when the biblical prophets were on the scene.

ZEPHANIAH

JOEL

HOSEA

HABAKKUK

800 BC   700 BC   650 BC

AMOS

OBADIAH

MEMORABLE WORDS
Seek me and live!
Amos 5:4

ISAIAH

NAHUM

JONAH

MICAH

BOOKS OF WISDOM

JOB
PSALMS
PROVERBS
ECCLESIASTES
SONG OF SONGS

* David wrote the most psalms (seventy-five), but six other named psalmists are in the book of Psalms. A large batch of psalms are anonymously written.[1]

MEMORABLE WORDS
"For I know the plans I have for you," declares the LORD, "plans to prosper you and not to harm you, plans to give you hope and a future."

Jeremiah 29:11 (NIV)

JEREMIAH

DANIEL

HAGGAI

* 445 BC Nehemiah rebuilds the walls of Jerusalem.

600 BC   500 BC   400 BC

LAMENTATIONS

* 515 BC The temple is rebuilt in Jerusalem.

MALACHI

EZEKIEL

ZECHARIAH

* There are approximately four hundred years between Malachi and the time of the Gospels.

* 586 BC Jerusalem falls to the Babylonians, and the temple is destroyed.

MEMORABLE WORDS
Trust in the LORD with all your heart, and do not lean on your own understanding. In all your ways acknowledge him, and he will make straight your paths.

Proverbs 3:5-6 (ESV)

Day 1

WISDOM FOR LIVING

If we were meeting face-to-face, I would give you a high five! We have covered a lot of ground over the past few weeks. From the creation to Israel returning from exile, you have walked through almost half of the Bible! Great job! This week we will take a break from the storyline. The books we will cover don't necessarily push forward the story of Scripture, but they do give us a glimpse into the experience of God's people living in relationship with Him.

The books of Job, Psalms, Proverbs, Ecclesiastes, and Song of Songs are all considered wisdom literature. To quote Patrick Schreiner, "the Wisdom Literature focuses on what it means to flourish, to be blessed, to prosper—to live this good life. Death is avoided and kingdom life is attained in three ways: (1) acquiring wisdom and following the [Law], (2) fearing the Lord, and (3) submitting to suffering. . . . The goal of the Wisdom Literature is to lead the people of Israel toward a life of flourishing."[1]

Historically, these books are describing events that for the most part took place at the same time as the events we discussed last week. So, Israel's monarchy, the fall of Jerusalem, exile, and the Israelites' return from exile are the inspiration for the words we will read. This week we will slow down and learn what it means to live with God during the in-between moments of joy, sorrow, anger, and celebration. But regardless of what moment in time they cover, each book seeks to answer the same question—*What does it mean to live as the people of God?*

Let's jump in!

READ JOB 1:1-3. Who was Job? Why was he so noteworthy?

We find out quickly that Job was a man of integrity and righteousness. The next four verses indicate that Job was wealthy and a caring father of several children. In fact, the end of verse 3 says he "was the greatest of all the people of the east" (ESV).

In Job 1:6–2:7, God gave His approval for Satan to test Job twice. Summarize the two ways in which Satan tested Job.

Why did God suggest Job to Satan?

1:8

2:3

What did Satan suggest God do to cause Job to curse God?

1:9-11

2:4-5

How did Satan afflict Job (and/or his family)?

1:12-19

2:6-7

How did Job respond?

1:20-22

2:8-10

In a short period of time, Job experienced a massive amount of suffering, losing all his children and his health. He had three friends who decided to come and support him, but alongside their support, they brought the assumption that Job was experiencing suffering because he deserved it. But Job vehemently denied any guilt. After almost thirty-seven chapters of discussion, God entered the conversation and cleared up the confusion among Job and his friends. In a world infected with sin, humanity will experience circumstances that are beyond our understanding. God does not always give us the answers we desire, and in those moments we have to humbly submit to the truth that God's ways and thoughts are above our own; we just have to learn to trust Him.[2]

READ JOB 42:1-6.

Why did Job apologize to God? Summarize Job's confession.

Have you walked through hard times that were difficult to understand and perhaps left you with unanswered questions? If so, how does Job's confession and testimony resonate with you?

It's easy to believe that life in the kingdom lived in obedience to the King will result in a life devoid of pain and suffering. But that is not the case because paradoxically the path to the kingdom is also a road of suffering. Job's story taught Israel, and also teaches us, that righteousness and suffering are not contradictory but two sides of the same coin.[3]

The book of Psalms is another book that gives voice to the paradoxes of life. Written by many different authors, including David and Moses, Psalms contains 150 songs that would serve as Israel's playlist during her journeys in and out of the land of Canaan. However, similar to the book of Proverbs, Psalms sets up the good life—the life of flourishing—as being connected with obedience to the law.

READ PSALM 1:1-6. Summarize the two different paths this psalm describes:

The Way of the R_____   The Way of the W_____

How does this psalm reiterate the wisdom Israel received from other leaders on how to walk in righteousness? Look back to Deuteronomy 6:4-8,17-19 for help with your answer.

The book of Psalms contains several different types, or genres, of psalms. There are psalms of thanksgiving, lament, celebration, imprecation (a psalm when the author calls for God to bring disaster or calamity on an enemy), and many more.[4] The psalms speak to both the joyous and the deeply painful moments of life, with the psalmist looking to find meaning and see God in every situation. The beauty of the psalms is that they don't rush past emotion but give space for our gamut of emotions to be felt and expressed before the Lord.

READ PSALM 13:1-6.

In this psalm of lament, what concerns did David bring before the Lord (vv. 1-2)?

How did David want God to respond to his concerns (vv. 3-4)?

In light of the first few verses, are David's words in verses 5-6 surprising? Explain why or why not.

Even in a place of lament, David ended his prayer to the Lord with praise. In some sense, this is indicative of the entirety of the book of Psalms. As we look at the book as a whole, the central affirmation of the psalter is that the Lord reigns.[5] Whether the psalmist was expressing bitter sorrow or exuberant joy, he was ultimately leading the reader to worship the Lord. The life of flourishing is one fully engaged in the worship of God, even during the hardest seasons.

READ PSALM 110:1-7. Who is the stated author of this psalm?

LOOK UP MATTHEW 26:64 AND MARK 14:62. To whom was the psalmist referring when he said, "my Lord" in Psalm 110:1? Circle the correct answer.

Himself   Jesus

In Psalm 110:2-3, what does the author tell us about this ruler's reign (e.g. His appearance, success in war, and extent of His kingdom)?

What promise from God does this psalm affirm (v. 4)? Look up Hebrews 5:5-6 for help with your answer.

Psalm 110 is a great example of how, in addition to calling God's people to worship, the psalms rehearsed the promises about Israel's king. Finding its fulfillment in Jesus, this psalm shows how the long-awaited Messianic King would be not only a son of David but his Lord. As they used this psalm and many others to rehearse the truth about their soon coming Deliverer, the people of Israel would renew their hope in God, knowing He would be faithful to fulfill His promises for salvation. To flourish in the kingdom is to both worship the King while living in eager expectation of His return!

Day 2

THE WAY OF FLOURISHING

The book of Proverbs is a collection of wise sayings compiled by King Solomon. He wrote some of them and then gathered others from his wise friends. Proverbs shows us how to live God's way in God's world. But as we read through this part of Scripture, we need to remember that proverbs are principles, not promises. For example, in Proverbs 15:1 we are told, "A gentle answer turns away anger, but a harsh word stirs up wrath." However, I have witnessed several instances when a believer responded in kindness and gentleness to an angry person only to be met with additional words of anger. So, even though these proverbs provide valuable wisdom for us, they aren't blanket guarantees; they are merely principles by which we can best live in God's world.

READ PROVERBS 1:1-7. Solomon gave several goals for writing the book of Proverbs. List three of them below.

1.

2.

3.

Look up the word *fear* in a dictionary and note any helpful synonyms you find that best fit with the context of Proverbs 1:7.

fear	

Based upon your answers, what does it mean to "fear the LORD" (v. 7)?

How is this type of fear "the beginning of knowledge" (v. 7)? Look up Psalm 111:10 to help with your answer.

Similar to Psalms, Proverbs begins by setting up two different pathways that people can take—the way of wisdom or the way of folly. There isn't a third option of neutrality; we either take one path or the other. The first few chapters of Proverbs give greater detail about both paths and then provide a series of statements that help readers walk in the way of wisdom in every area of their lives. Whether it's with our emotions, speech, money, relationships, or virtue, Solomon shows us that to flourish is to follow the way of wisdom. And the door that leads us there is a fear of God that recognizes He alone is perfectly holy, righteous, and just.[6] Only by following Him can we be formed into the kind of people who experience true flourishing in His kingdom.

If Proverbs focuses on the regularities of life, Ecclesiastes focuses on the anomalies.[7] You don't have to live long to realize that those who faithfully follow God still experience hardship, death, sorrow, injustice, and poverty. The tragedies of life do not skip over our doorstep simply because we are the people of God. In Ecclesiastes, Solomon sought to make sense of this paradox as he searched for the meaning of life.

READ ECCLESIASTES 1:12-18.

What did Solomon devote himself to as king of Israel?

What truth did Solomon realize at the end of his search?

Remember what we learned about Solomon in 1 Kings? He was a man who had everything—money, women, prestige, wisdom, and knowledge. People came from all over to learn from him. But as we read through Ecclesiastes, we will see Solomon discover how none of those things protected a person from the irregularities of life. In his words, "I have seen all the things that are done under the sun and have found everything to be futile . . ." (Eccl. 1:14a).

I don't know about you, but these words don't seem too hopeful. For this reason, it can be hard to reconcile what Solomon said with what we have read in the other wisdom books. How do Solomon's words lead us to the life of flourishing?

Let's check out what he said at the end of Ecclesiastes.

> **READ ECCLESIASTES 12:13-14.** After searching for the meaning of life, what was Solomon's final conclusion, and how does it connect to what he wrote in Proverbs 1:7?

Having all that life could give to any one person, Solomon realized that ultimate meaning was not found in possessions, intellect, or experiences but in God. He was not trying to ignore the realities of life that don't make sense or the tragic experiences that cause us deep sorrow but to show how we are unable to control any of it. Our ultimate hope and source of flourishing is found only by living to worship our Lord and King. In the midst of what is unsure and seemingly fleeting, He brings the life and hope we long for.

> How does this truth line up with the narratives that our current culture is promoting?

The last book of wisdom literature is Song of Songs. I'll be honest—I haven't heard many sermon series on this book or read many devotionals about it. I think for most people, Song of Songs feels a bit awkward, like we need to whisper anytime we talk about it. The reason for this is that much of Song of Songs discusses the intimate, sexual details of a relationship between the king and his bride. At first glance, this book seems to be out of place, not fitting within this storyline of kingdom and flourishing. But as we take a few moments to review its contents, I think we will see that it does in fact fit, proclaiming the same message of wisdom we've studied this week.

READ SONG OF SONGS 1:1-17.

Describe the tone of the conversation between the young woman and the young man. What physical aspects of each other do they celebrate? List them below.

Based upon their conversation, what value should the people of God place on marriage and sex within marriage?

In what way should our view of both these things be connected to our worship of God?

Through a series of love poems, Song of Songs presents the emotions that accompany the days leading up to and during marriage. The marital relationship is a gift that should point us toward the goodness and beauty of God. The life of flourishing is holistic and includes the enjoyment of God's blessings, specifically the sexual union between a husband and a wife. But even though Song of Songs leads us to include the enjoyment of marriage within the way of wisdom, we can't fail to recognize that marriage is fleeting. So, these beautiful love poems also point to something greater, a relationship with Someone greater, a relationship with Someone that will never end. The love of Christ and His church fit within the theme of Song of Songs.[8]

The way of wisdom shows us that God's people flourish when they are in relationship with the King. This relationship is one of goodness and beauty that will be enjoyed forever.

Day 3

THE SEERS SPEAK

This week we are slowing down and learning about what it's like to live in God's kingdom as His people. Over the past two days, we have focused on the topic of wisdom, or how to live God's way in God's world. The Wisdom books show us that the good life—the life of flourishing—follows the way of our Lord and King. To live well and be blessed in the kingdom is to follow the King's rule. Even when life does not turn out the way we hope, the greatest blessing we have is to be in the presence of the King. Most of the words of wisdom we read these past two days were written during the years of Israel's monarchy, during exile, and after the people returned home. But we know that during this season of Israel's history, the Israelites struggled to walk in the way of wisdom, hanging out with their foreign neighbors and worshiping their gods.

The next set of books we'll cover continues the theme of life in the kingdom but focuses on the messengers God sent to Israel to remind them of their covenant with Him. These messengers are called prophets, or in the words of Vaughan Roberts, "covenant enforcers." The role of prophets was to implore the people to obey the covenant, reminding them of the blessings that would come from obedience and the curses from disobedience.[9] They often prophesied about future events that were related to Israel's obedience or disobedience to the covenant. They spoke of consequences but also gave Israel encouragement, reminding the people of the hope of their promised King.

The prophetic books are also categorized as either Major or Minor Prophets. The categories aren't based on the value of their messages but on the size of the book.

Rather than cover every prophetic book individually, we will talk about them according to the themes they address and the season of Israel's history they cover. There are three major seasons of prophecy in the life of Israel—before exile, during exile, and after exile. As covenant enforcers, these prophets spoke both of judgment and hope. Today we will talk about their message of judgment and tomorrow their message of hope.

Take a look at the chart below. Then, using your Bible's table of contents, highlight in green the first five books that come after Song of Songs. Highlight the subsequent twelve books in yellow.

Pre-Exilic		Exile	Post-Exilic
Hosea Joel Amos Obadiah Jonah	Isaiah Micah Nahum Habakkuk Zephaniah	Ezekiel Daniel	Haggai Zechariah Malachi
Jeremiah Lamentations			

Israel was supposed to be a light to the nations, a kingdom of priests, and a holy nation showing those around how to worship the one true God. But the people of Israel had forgotten why God delivered them out of Egypt and gave them the land and His law. Instead of being characterized by faithfulness and love, Israel participated in idolatry, flagrant social injustice, and religious syncretism (mixing pagan religious practices with their worship of God).[10] Much of the writings of the pre-exilic prophets is dedicated to calling out this behavior to move Israel back to covenant faithfulness.

READ AMOS 2:6-8; 5:11-13,21-27.

What was Israel guilty of doing? In what way were the Israelites mistreating people in their community?

How did God respond to their behavior? What did God desire more than their religious activity (i.e., sacrifice)? Why?

Do you ever find yourself in a similar situation as Israel? Explain. How do you find your way back to spiritual authenticity?

As the people of God, the Israelites were responsible for stewarding God's kingdom for the flourishing of all creation and humanity. But rather than seeking the best for other image bearers, the Israelites were taking advantage of the most vulnerable in their communities for personal gain. To dishonor image bearers is to dishonor the One whose image they bear. Injustice is an offense to God because it disregards the care we are supposed to have for His creation and the honor we have for Him. So, Israel's worship of God was a farce, and through the prophets, God made it clear He would not be worshiped and known apart from a commitment to justice.[11]

READ JEREMIAH 2:26-28 AND HOSEA 4:12.

What was Israel accused of in these passages?

In what way did the prophets mock their actions? Explain why.

In addition to social injustice, Israel was guilty of worshiping idols. The problem wasn't just that Israel was worshiping physical images of gods made out of wood or stone but that her love and allegiance were misplaced. The people of Israel had forgotten the God who delivered them out of Egypt and were looking to these foreign gods as sources of protection and provision. The Israelites wouldn't leave behind their worship of God completely but would try to worship God and their foreign gods at the same time. But the foreign gods couldn't compare or match up to the one true God. The prophet Jeremiah said it like this, "For my people have committed a double evil: They have abandoned me, the fountain of living water, and dug cisterns for themselves—cracked cisterns that cannot hold water" (Jer. 2:13).

READ AMOS 2:4-5,11.

What was the future judgment that the prophet Amos proclaimed to Judah and Israel?

Why did God punish the entire nation and not just the individual people who were guilty of sinful behavior?

How do these verses connect with the words of Moses in Deuteronomy 4:21-31?

As a community, Israel was interconnected, which means that one person's sin would impact the entire nation.[12] So, to reinforce this communal identity and to provide a strong deterrent to sin, God would judge *all* of Israel many times, not only the individual person who was guilty of sin. God showed His patience through the message of the prophets, giving the Israelites a long time to repent and return to living as His people in obedience to the covenant. But He was also faithful, upholding the promises of judgment He made to Israel, even as far back as Moses. He promised He would send Israel into exile if the people failed to obey the covenant, and He did.

LOOK BACK TO DEUTERONOMY 4:30-31. What did God promise Israel after a season of exile?

Today we talked a lot about judgment, which might have felt a bit heavy. But take a deep breath! Tomorrow we will talk about the hope of salvation that the prophets proclaimed to Israel. Even while the Israelites were experiencing the consequences of their sin, the prophets gave them hope that God had not abandoned His promise to bless them.

Day 4

THE KING WILL COME

For Israel, exile was catastrophic. Both the Northern Kingdom of Israel and the Southern Kingdom of Judah were attacked and conquered by foreign nations. Israel fell in 722 BC to the Assyrians, and Judah was laid waste by the Babylonians in 586 BC. Both conquering nations were ruthless, destroying Israel's cities, killing their people, and taking those that were left as slaves. The devastation was disastrous, especially in the Southern Kingdom where the beloved temple in Jerusalem was burned to the ground. The place where God had dwelled with His people was no more, and God's people were marched off into exile. Life in the Kingdom was dreadful.

READ LAMENTATIONS 1:1-4.

This book of lament was written by Jeremiah after Judah was taken into exile by Babylon. He started by describing the difference between the nation before exile and after being taken into exile.

Summarize what he said in the chart below.

Before Exile	After Exile

List the synonyms for *lament* that Jeremiah used in these verses.

The devastation of Jerusalem was awful. But while the people felt as if God had forgotten them, the opposite was true. Even though He had enacted the judgment they were experiencing, the judgment was a means to an end. After seventy years, God would bring them back to the land He had promised them (Jer. 25; Dan. 9).

Many of the prophets reminded Israel of this message of hope, especially when they were in exile. The prophets helped the people of Israel stay faithful to God while they waited on His deliverance.

READ ISAIAH 43:1-5.

In Isaiah 43:1, the Lord used three verbs to explain His relationship to Israel. List them below.

1.

2.

3.

Considering His judgment of Israel, why do you think the Lord used these words to identify Himself to Israel?

What did He promise Israel (v. 2)? Also look to Isaiah 8:7-8; 29:6 for help with your answer.

What was the motivation for making this promise (43:3)?

I can't imagine what the people of Israel must have thought and felt as they were dragged away from their homeland. Fear, uncertainty, grief, anger, and many other emotions probably filled their hearts and minds as they made the trek to Assyria and Babylon. Furthermore, Israel would stay in exile for a long time.

Those who had been exiled to Babylon would be there for seventy years, and those who had been exiled to Assyria never came back home.

Even though they felt like God had abandoned them, He had not. Throughout their time in exile, God used the prophets to give the people hope. Despite their current circumstances, God kept His promises, both for deliverance out of captivity and for salvation through the promised King.

READ JEREMIAH 29:4-14.

Describe the instructions God gave the Israelites for how they were supposed to live in exile.

Why might Israel have been tempted to listen to false prophets while in exile?

What message of hope did God give Israel in verses 10-14? What was He promising to restore?

God's promise of deliverance for Israel was connected to the covenants He made with Abraham, Moses, and David. He was promising to bring them back to the land of Canaan, back under His rule and blessing. But even when the people of Israel came out of exile, they still struggled with the same problem they had before exile—sin. We read about this during our journey through Ezra and Nehemiah. After Israel returned to their homeland, they struggled to stay faithful to the covenant. The people of Israel needed a solution that would enable them to be faithful forever.

READ JEREMIAH 32:37-41 AND EZEKIEL 11:19-20.

What type of transformation would the Israelites experience after they returned to the promised land?

What would this transformation enable them to do?

God knew His people needed help, a permanent solution to the problem that had been plaguing them since the garden of Eden. Through both the prophet Jeremiah and the prophet Ezekiel, God made one more covenant with Israel. He promised to cleanse the people, curing them of their disease of sin. This new covenant would include a full forgiveness of sins; God would remember their sin no more.[13] Israel and all of the nations would live in restored relationship with God in His kingdom (Isa. 56:4-8).

The prophets spoke triumphantly of this future day of permanent restoration and also talked about the King from the line of David who would be the means through which the new covenant would come.

MESSIAH means "anointed one." Israel's use of this term was closely tied to the promises of the Davidic Covenant. For them, the "Messiah" was the promised King whose kingdom would endure forever (2 Sam. 7:16).

READ THE VERSES ON THE NEXT PAGE. Match them to the correct messianic prophecy.

a. Psalm 16:10	The Messiah would be exalted at God's right hand.
b. Psalm 110:1	The Messiah would be sold for thirty pieces of silver.
c. Isaiah 7:14	The Messiah would perform miracles.
d. Isaiah 8:14	The Messiah would be despised and rejected.
e. Isaiah 35:5-6	The Messiah would rise from the dead.
f. Isaiah 53:3	The Messiah would be a stone that would cause people to stumble.
g. Micah 5:2	The Messiah would be born in Bethlehem.
h. Zechariah 11:12	The Messiah would be born of a virgin.

In 538 BC, the exiles were allowed to return home. Cyrus of Persia defeated the Babylonians and issued an edict that allowed the people to return to Jerusalem to rebuild the temple. However, only a small number returned. Under the leadership of Ezra and Nehemiah, they experienced opposition while they were rebuilding the temple and the city walls. Life was not easy, and the Israelites ended up falling into the same sin patterns that sent them into exile. Like their predecessors, the three post-exilic prophets, Haggai, Zechariah, and Malachi, preached messages of judgment and hope to Israel. They reminded Israel of the covenant, the blessings for obedience, and curses for disobedience.

At the end of the last book of the Old Testament, Malachi, we are left waiting for the fulfillment of God's promises. Israel was back in her homeland, but spiritually speaking the people were still in exile waiting for God to fulfill His promise of salvation. God's kingdom still had not come because God's King had not come. But the words of Malachi leave the people with hope that the King will appear (Mal. 3:1-4). God had not forgotten His promise. He would restore His kingdom, and through His King, He would establish it over the whole earth.

Day 5

WEEKLY REVIEW

This week we walked through our fifth session of the grand narrative of Scripture, where we learned about what life was like in the kingdom from both wisdom literature and the prophets. Answer the questions below to summarize this week's main points. Feel free to use bullet points.

1. What is wisdom? What two life paths does wisdom literature talk about?

2. What is the difference between Psalms and Proverbs?

3. What was the role of a prophet? During what three periods did the prophets minister to Israel?

4. What were the main accusations of the prophets against Israel? What did they say God would do if Israel did not repent?

5. How did the prophets provide Israel with hope? In whom was this hope rooted?

SUMMARIZE THE NARRATIVE

In the space below, use your answers to the previous questions to create a two to three sentence summary of what happened this session in the grand narrative of Scripture.

Video + Group Guide

SESSION FIVE

To access the video teaching sessions, use the instructions in the back of your Bible study book.

WATCH Session Five video teaching and take notes below.

DISCUSSION QUESTIONS

1   What is the message of the book of Job? Can you relate to his story? Explain.

2   What does it mean for God to be sovereign? How does that affect your daily life?

3   What is your favorite psalm? Why?

4   What is a proverb? How does Proverbs help you in your walk with the Lord?

5   What was the role of the prophets? Does anyone fill that kind of role today? Explain.

6   What is one point or truth that really stood out to you from the video teaching? Why?

THE STATUS OF THE KINGDOM

In the chart below, fill in the blanks to review the definition of the kingdom of God. (Look back at your notes on p. 13 if you need help). At the close of each teaching video, I will update the status of each phrase.

The Kingdom of God	Life in the Kingdom
God's _____ in	
God's _____ under	
God's _____ and _____.	

SESSION SIX

The Arrival of the King

Timeline
SESSION SIX

MEMORABLE WORDS

The Spirit of the Lord is on me, because he has anointed me to preach good news to the poor. He has sent me to proclaim release to the captives and recovery of sight to the blind, to set free the oppressed, to proclaim the year of the Lord's favor.

Luke 4:18-19

JESUS IS BORN

* Although we celebrate Jesus's birth on December 25, it's highly unlikely that was the day He was born. The actual date is unknown. In fact, even the year He was born is uncertain. Scholars think it was sometime between 6 BC and 4 BC.[1]

5 BC

AD 20

MEMORABLE WORDS

Behold, the Lamb of God!

John 1:36 (ESV)

JOHN THE BAPTIST ON THE SCENE

BOOKS

MATTHEW

MARK

LUKE

JOHN

* Jesus had several half-siblings (Matt. 13:55-56). His half-brother James became a leader in the Jerusalem church and is thought to have written the letter of James.

FUN FACT

Jesus's hometown was Nazareth, a small village in Galilee. Today, Nazareth has a population of around eighty thousand.[2]

* Jesus's only miracle found in all four Gospels is the feeding of the five thousand.

JESUS BEGINS MINISTRY

JESUS'S DEATH

AD 25

AD 33

PASSION WEEK

JESUS'S RESURRECTION

JESUS'S 12 DISCIPLES

* Simon Peter
* James
* John
* Andrew
* Philip
* Bartholomew
* Matthew
* Thomas
* James, the son of Alphaeus
* Thaddaeus
* Simon the Zealot
* Judas Iscariot
(Mark 3:16-19)

* Passion Week (also called Holy Week) was the week before Jesus's death. It started with His triumphal entry into Jerusalem and concluded with His resurrection.

MEMORABLE WORDS
Why do you seek the living among the dead? He is not here, but has risen.
Luke 24:5-6 (ESV)

Day 1

THE KING IS BORN

In our Bibles, as we turn the page from Malachi to Matthew, it's easy to forget that there is over four hundred years of history between these two books.

Just think about that for a moment. At the end of Malachi, we left Israel desperately hoping for God to send the promised Savior. But for hundreds and hundreds of years, He didn't. But the Israelites didn't stop believing.[1] Many waited faithfully for their Savior to come.

Theologians call the historical period between Malachi and Matthew the Intertestamental Period. During this time, Israel remained under the rule of pagan nations. While a small number of the Jewish exiles had returned to their homeland, many were still scattered around the Roman Empire. The promises God made to Abraham, Moses, and David included a united Israel. So as they lived under foreign oppression, the people of Israel waited eagerly for the day in which God, through the promised king, would unite them, restoring the kingdom of God.

As they waited, the Jews prayed, learned the Law (the Torah), celebrated their religious festivals, and gathered at their places of worship (aka synagogues) to remind themselves of the covenant they had made with God. With about half a million Jews living in Israel and about three million scattered across the Roman Empire, most looked for a day when God would return to redeem His people from their pagan oppressors.[2] They didn't know God was going to do so much more. His work of restoration would eradicate sin, Satan, and death from the world, bringing the whole of creation and humankind once again under God's gracious rule.[3] Salvation would come when the king arrived. So they waited in hope.

And then one day, Hope came.

READ MATTHEW 1:1. The author, Matthew, gave Jesus two important titles. List them below and then explain why they are significant. Look up Genesis 12:1-3 and 2 Samuel 7:1-16 to help with your answer.

Title	Significance of the Title
1. Son of _____	
2. Son of _____	

In his opening words, Matthew proclaimed the good news that the promised King had come! Written to a primarily Jewish audience, Matthew traced Jesus's lineage, showing how He came from the family line of David and Abraham. With the arrival of the King, God's promises of kingdom restoration would be fulfilled. This was an epic moment for Israel (and for us)! Even though the Israelites had waited a long time, God had not forgotten them.

Matthew is one of four Gospels that each tell the story about the arrival of King Jesus! Each Gospel paints a unique portrait of Jesus Christ, providing special insight into who He is and what He accomplished. The Gospels exhibit both unity and diversity, bearing witness to the same Jesus (unity) but viewing Him from unique perspectives (diversity).

Like we did with the books of prophecy, we will not go through each Gospel individually but look at them as a whole. We will focus on the events the books discuss and then see how each of the Gospels presents that part of Jesus's life. Today we will discuss Jesus's birth. For the rest of the week, we will examine His ministry, message, and death/burial/resurrection.

MATTHEW wrote to Jewish-Christian communities struggling with their relationship to Judaism. He stressed the fulfillment of Old Testament prophecies to show that Jesus is the Jewish Messiah.

MARK portrayed Jesus as the suffering Son of God who offers Himself as a sacrifice for sins. His Gospel is often associated with the persecuted church in Rome.

LUKE pictured Jesus as Savior who brings salvation to all nations and people groups.

JOHN showed Jesus as the eternal Son of God, the self-revelation of God the Father. John's original audience consisted of both Jews and Gentiles living in the larger Greco-Roman world.

READ MATTHEW 1:18-25.

In Matthew 1:18, the word *engaged* is also translated as "betrothed." Betrothal was similar to our modern-day engagement, except it was as binding as marriage.

What happened after Mary and Joseph got engaged? Read Luke 1:26-38 for help with your answer.

How did Joseph respond?

What title did the angel use to address Joseph in Matthew 1:20? Explain why.

The angel referred to the coming Son by two different names. List them below along with the meaning of each name.

1. Verse 21

2. Verse 23

Mary and Joseph lived in a time period when having a child outside of wedlock was not socially accepted. I wonder what went through Joseph's mind when Mary told him she was pregnant—by the Holy Spirit! Joseph had every right to make a public spectacle of Mary, but he decided to handle the situation quietly, preserving Mary's honor and dignity. But before he took any action, the same God that spoke through an angel to Mary did the same with Joseph. The angel's words assured Joseph that not only was Mary telling the truth, but the baby she was carrying was the promised Messianic King!

READ LUKE 2:1-7.

Why did Joseph and Mary leave Nazareth to go to Bethlehem?

What messianic prophecy did this fulfill? Look back to Session Five, Day Four for help with this question.

Describe the conditions of Jesus's birth. How might Jesus's birth have differed from what Jews were expecting of their promised King?

When Jesus was born, only His parents and maybe a few animals were there to welcome Him. That's it. There was no fanfare, loud celebrations, or military processional. The moment of His introduction into the world is not what we would expect for the birth of a King. Rather than coming in power and grandeur, the promised King was born in humility and poverty.

READ LUKE 2:8-20.

Who was among the first to hear about the birth of Jesus? Explain why this is significant.

The angel said his message was good news of great joy. Who was this message intended for, and how did the angel confirm his message was indeed good news (vv. 10-11)?

What were the responses of the people who heard the message of the angel?

The shepherds (vv. 15-17,20)

All who heard it (v. 18)

Mary (v. 19)

In Matthew 2, we learn that not everyone who heard about the birth of Jesus was pleased with the news. When the wise men followed the star to Jerusalem and asked about the newborn king and their desire to worship Him, Herod was disturbed (v. 3). He didn't appreciate this threat to his power. So he instructed the wise men to let him know exactly where this new King was located after they found Him. But God was protecting this baby King. He warned the wise men to return home by a different route and told Joseph to take Mary and Jesus to Egypt. When Herod realized he'd been outwitted by the wise men, he tried to end Jesus's life by having every male child in Bethlehem two years old and under killed.

READ MATTHEW 2:19-20.

What was God's instruction to Joseph after Herod's death?

What previous moment in the life of Israel comes to mind when you read this passage in Matthew?

Similar to God preserving His people by rescuing them from slavery in Egypt and leading them to the promised land, He told Joseph to leave Egypt to go back to Nazareth. While this would not be the last time someone would try to kill Jesus, the mission of the King would not be thwarted. The angelic celebration of His birth was rooted in the overwhelming realization that God's long-awaited promise for kingdom restoration was being fulfilled. Even though Israel was currently in spiritual exile, Jesus's life and ministry would be used to unite the kingdom, defeat sin and death, and bring the blessing of God to all of humanity.

But as we will see tomorrow, not everyone was receptive to Jesus's ministry because life in the kingdom under the rule of this King didn't look like they thought it would.

Day 2

THE MINISTRY BEGINS

The biblical authors didn't tell us much about Jesus's childhood. Other than one situation when His parents mistakenly left Him behind in Jerusalem and found Him in the temple "sitting among the teachers, listening to them and asking them questions" (Luke 2:46), they skipped over His younger years and picked up at the point when He began His ministry. Most of the Gospel authors didn't begin with Jesus's ministry but with the ministry of John the Baptist.

John the Baptist was the son of Zechariah and Elizabeth. His miraculous birth (Zechariah and Elizabeth were both advanced in years and didn't have any children because she was barren) was foretold to Zechariah by an angel, who also explained that John would be the forerunner of the Messiah (Luke 1:5-25). We find out in Jesus's birth story that Elizabeth was related to Mary (Luke 1:35-36). How they were related is not defined, but it was to Elizabeth's house that Mary traveled after she found out she was pregnant with Jesus (Luke 1:39-45).

John the Baptist came onto the scene out in the wilderness with a fiery ministry and message.

> **READ LUKE 3:3-9.** Luke quoted Isaiah 40:3-5 in his description of John. How was John's ministry a fulfillment of this prophecy?

As a result of his message and ministry, the crowds thought John could be the Messiah. But he differentiated himself by letting them know that someone else was coming after him who would be much greater. While John baptized the people with water, he told them the Messiah would baptize them with the Holy Spirit and fire. He also spoke of the judgment that the Messiah would bring to those who lived in opposition to the King.

The day after John gave this message, the One who is greater came to meet him.

READ JOHN 1:29-34.

What title did John give Jesus? In what way would Jesus fulfill the prophecy of Isaiah 53:7?

What did John testify about Jesus?

During the baptism of Jesus, God the Father uttered the words, "You are my beloved Son; with you I am well pleased" (Luke 3:22). With these words, God the Father affirmed that Jesus was Israel's anointed King, here to fulfill God's kingdom plan of restoration. And the Holy Spirit, who descended on Jesus like a dove, would empower Jesus to carry out this plan, which included the salvation of all humanity.[4] But before Jesus began His public ministry, He was led into the wilderness by the Holy Spirit for a forty-day fast. As soon as His fast was over, Satan tempted Him.

READ MATTHEW 4:1-11.

Satan tried to entice Jesus with three separate temptations. In your own words, summarize each temptation and how Jesus responded.

1.

2.

3.

Note that Jesus used Scripture to combat each of Satan's temptations. Instead of giving in to Satan's tempting promises of food, glory, and power, by the power of the Holy Spirit, Jesus chose the road of sacrifice. Even in His weakened state, Jesus made a choice that would characterize the rest of His ministry. His focus would be on doing the work of His Father, and nothing, even His physical pain, suffering, or hunger would get in the way.

After Jesus was affirmed by the Father at His baptism and strengthened by the Holy Spirit in the wilderness, Jesus humbly began His ministry to make known the kingdom of God. Throughout His ministry travels, Jesus would announce that the kingdom John the Baptist had prophesied about had come. While we will talk about it more tomorrow, Jesus announced the good news that God's power to save creation had arrived. God entered human history in love and power to liberate, heal, and restore the world.[5] Some who merely heard Jesus's words would believe Him, but others would be convinced through the miraculous works He performed that both authenticated His authority and validated His message.

READ THE FOLLOWING PASSAGES. Then name the miracle and what it displayed Jesus had authority over.

Passage	The Miracle	Jesus's Authority
Mark 1:21-28		
Mark 4:35-41		
Luke 7:11-17		
Luke 18:35-43		

Through His miracles, Jesus displayed He had power over everything, including demonic powers, sickness, nature, and even death.

The ministry of Jesus is kingdom restoration. He brings life, healing, and peace into a world ravaged by sin. During His ministry, Jesus gave people glimpses of the kingdom. In God's kingdom, sickness, pain, and death are no more, and the creation is restored to its original beauty and harmony.[6] Remember, sin is an intruder. It was never intended to be a part of God's creation. Through His miracles, Jesus gives humanity a quick picture of a world that is devoid of sin.

But Jesus's ministry did not only include miracles. It also included a clear message about what it meant to live in the kingdom, and it would prove to be a message that would get Him killed.

Day 3

THE MASTER TEACHER

I believe many people overlook the significance of the moment in history that Jesus lived on earth. He was born under the rule of the Roman Empire. In the days of Jesus, Roman emperors were thought to be Lord and the son of God. So when Jesus was announcing the coming of the kingdom, He was proclaiming Himself to be the true Ruler of the world. This wasn't a statement that could be met with neutrality; it required a response. And the response Jesus required was one of allegiance.

READ MATTHEW 4:17 AND MARK 1:15-17.

Look up the word *repent* in a dictionary and then write a definition for it below that fits its context in both verses.

> **repent**

Based on your definition, what was Jesus asking His listeners to do?

After He proclaimed His message of repentance, Jesus invited a group of fishermen to follow Him. How was this action different from repentance? Give your best answer; we will cover it in the video teaching time.

During the time of Jesus, discipleship "primarily involved commitment of an individual to a great master or leader."[7] In the same way, Jesus's model of discipleship required His followers to commit to Him and the standard of kingdom living He required. As with other forms of discipleship in the ancient world, Jesus's disciples should have been able to be distinctly identified by their unique behavior. Their actions and perspectives were to reflect allegiance to Jesus as their Master and Leader. With His call to repent, believe, and follow, Jesus was asking people to reject their false stories and learn to live as He did.[8]

However, Jesus was not like any other rabbi. To follow Him was not an invitation to follow another "good teacher." Jesus is Lord and King, so His threefold invitation was ultimately a call for allegiance—to be loyal to the rule of Jesus. And through His preaching, Jesus showed His followers what it looks like to live in allegiance to the King.

READ MATTHEW 5:3-20.

Look up the word *blessed* in a dictionary and write a definition for it that fits its context in this passage.

blessed	

In the following chart, write the phrase the Amplified Bible uses to describe each category of blessedness that Jesus stated in the beatitudes.

The Blessed (CSB)	The Blessed (AMP)
the poor in spirit	those devoid of spiritual arrogance, those who regard themselves as insignificant
those who mourn	
those who are humble	

those who hunger and thirst for righteousness	
those who are merciful	
those who are pure in heart	
those who are peacemakers	
those who are persecuted because of righteousness	

How does comparing the categories in the CSB and AMP help you understand what Jesus was saying about blessedness in the kingdom of God?

In Matthew 5:13-14, Jesus used salt and light as metaphors for how citizens of the kingdom of God should live. What does it mean for kingdom citizens to be the salt of the earth?

READ ISAIAH 42:6-7.

How do these verses clarify your understanding of what it means for kingdom citizens to be the light of the world?

What are some practical ways you can be salt and light to the world around you?

Jesus would have grown up using the Hebrew Bible, which only included the books of the Old Testament. The Hebrew Bible also organized the Old Testament books in a different order than our English Bible. So when Jesus was talking about the Law and the Prophets in Matthew 5:17, He was referring to the books of the Bible that detail Israel's history, specifically: Genesis, Exodus, Leviticus, Numbers, Deuteronomy, Joshua, Judges, 1 and 2 Samuel, 1 and 2 Kings, Isaiah, Jeremiah, Ezekiel, and the Minor Prophets.

From what you remember about these books, how did Jesus fulfill the law? (Hint: Think back to the series of promises God made to Israel.)

What did Jesus say is the righteousness requirement for entrance into the kingdom of heaven?

The kingdom living that Jesus talked about was much different than the values of the world in which Jesus lived. In Jesus's upside-down kingdom, to be first was to be last, to be greatest was to be the least, and to be exalted was to be humble. The most vulnerable, marginalized, and overlooked members of society were not cast aside but welcomed into the kingdom. Jesus got in a lot of trouble during His time on earth because He hung out with sinners and outcasts. He rejected the elitism and legalism of the Jewish religious leaders. True kingdom living was characterized by a love for God that was evidenced by a self-sacrificial love for one's neighbor (Matt. 5:43-45).

But sometimes, Jesus's disciples had a difficult time understanding Jesus's message about the kingdom of God. So, Jesus would often use parables to make His message clearer to them and more confusing to others.

READ MATTHEW 13:24-30,36-43. Jesus provided seven key details in His clarification of this parable. List them in the chart below.

Matthew 13:24-30	Jesus's Explanation in Matthew 13:36-43
Who is the sower?	
Who is the field?	
Who is the seed?	
Who are the weeds?	
Who is the enemy?	
When is the harvest?	
Who are the harvesters?	

Jesus used parables to tell people truths about the kingdom of God. In the parable about the sower and the seed; He showed how the kingdom is both "already" and "not yet." With the coming of the kings, the Jews expected the present evil age to pass away quickly. The parable of the sower teaches how the power of evil continues alongside the power of healing that has come into the world through Jesus. Even though the King has come, sin and death are still present in the world, but one day "the weeds" will be harvested and evil will be no more.

Through Jesus's other parables, we learn how the beauty of the King and His kingdom is demonstrated in humility, not dominance (Luke 14:7-14). We also learn that the kingdom is given, not earned (Mark 10:13-16). Entrance into the kingdom comes only through us "admitting that we have nothing to give, that all we can do is rely on Christ for grace and forgiveness."[9] The kingdom of God exists through the kingdom community who are demonstrating the message of the King in love, deed, and truth.

Tomorrow, as we walk through the final moments of Jesus's ministry on earth, we will uncover one final insight into the kingdom of God—the victory of the King comes not through military power but by His death on the cross.

Day 4

THE KING GIVES HIS LIFE

Jesus spent the last three years of His earthly life ministering, preaching the message of the kingdom of God, and inviting people to follow Him. His journeys eventually led Him to His final ministry location—Jerusalem during Passover. Throughout His ministry, Jesus experienced opposition to His message. By declaring Himself as Lord and King, Jesus made a bold claim that did not sit well with the Jewish religious leaders. But their attempts to silence the King of creation actually did the opposite. As a part of God's divine plan, Jesus's crucifixion and resurrection serve as His enthronement, confirming Him as King and claiming final victory for the kingdom of God.

READ MATTHEW 21:1-11.

What did Jesus ask the disciples to do?

Why did Jesus decide to enter the city this way? In what way is this a fulfillment of Zechariah 9:9?

Describe the difference between how the people in the crowd and the people in the city responded to Jesus.

In Zechariah 9, the prophet spoke of Israel's King returning to Jerusalem after a military victory.[10] There had been other victory parades for triumphant kings and generals in Israel's history. So when Jesus rode the donkey into the city,

He was making it very clear He was the Davidic King and Messiah. But Jesus came as a gentle and humble King, not with a great show of military power. This means that even though some clearly recognized His kingship, they misunderstood the nature of His rule. Within days, this same crowd would not be shouting Jesus's praises but demanding He be nailed to a cross.[11]

Jesus entered Jerusalem a week before His death. After entering the city, He went to visit the temple, the epicenter of life for the Jews. The people saw the temple as the place where God dwelled. The Jews believed that when their Messianic King arrived, He would return to the temple to judge the pagan Gentiles and the Jews who had been unfaithful to God by engaging in pagan religious practices.[12] But because the Israelites misunderstood Jesus's kingship and teaching, they did not know they were the ones who would be objects of God's judgment (Mark 12–13).

The temple was supposed to be the place where Israel met with God and where the people of Israel showed the nations how to worship the one true God (Isa. 56:7). But instead of providing a space for the nations to worship, the Jews used that space as a market. The "house of prayer" had turned into a den of robbers because the Jewish merchants were robbing the Gentiles of their rightful claim to worship. The Jews had forgotten their role as a kingdom of priests and a holy nation. Judgment on this temple had to take place so that a new temple, Jesus's resurrection life in the renewed people of God, could become the light for the nations that God intended.[13]

> **READ MATTHEW 26:17-30.** What was Passover? Look back to Exodus 12:12-28 for help with your answer.

During the Passover Meal, the Jews would retell the history of their exodus while looking forward to the new exodus when the Messianic King would come and deliver them out of exile. But Jesus gave this meal new meaning, letting the disciples know that the kingdom Israel longed for had come through Him.[14]

PASSOVER was a yearly celebration when the Israelites would remember their deliverance out of slavery in Egypt. The annual Passover meal would include bread and wine.

The bread was a reminder of the unleavened bread the people of Israel took with them when they left Egypt (Ex. 12:34).

The wine was a reminder of how, in the final plague, God passed over the Israelite houses that were sprinkled with the blood of a sacrificial lamb (Ex. 12:13).

In the following chart, describe the new meaning He gave to the meal elements.

Meal Element	New Meaning
Bread	
Cup	

At this moment, Jesus was predicting His death. His mission to conquer sin and restore the kingdom was about to be fulfilled. Soon, Jesus would bring the deliverance Israel eagerly anticipated, but the Israelites' deliverance would come through His death.

After the Passover meal, the opposition to Jesus's ministry reached its climax. Betrayed by Judas Iscariot, one of His disciples, Jesus was arrested and brought before the Sanhedrin (the religious leadership of Israel) under the charge of blasphemy. Through His actions and words during His ministry journey, Jesus proclaimed to be the Son of God and the promised Messiah (Luke 4:18-21; John 4:25-26), and either He was telling the truth or He was lying. The Sanhedrin chose to believe the second option. But the Jews did not have the power to put anyone to death, so they brought Jesus before Pilate (a Roman official), and accused Jesus of the capital offense of treason.

READ LUKE 23:13-25.

After Pilate investigated the charges against Jesus, did he declare Jesus to be guilty or innocent? Explain.

How did the crowd respond to Pilate's decision?

Pilate unsuccessfully tried to release Jesus. He realized Jesus had done nothing deserving of death. But the crowd continued to press him. He tried to satisfy them by having Jesus whipped. But the crowd would have none of it. He tried to release Jesus by using a traditional Passover custom of freeing one prisoner by popular demand (Matt. 27:15). He pitted Jesus versus Barabbas, "a notorious prisoner" (Matt. 27:16), thinking surely the crowd would choose Jesus. But the crowd chose Barabbas and continued to cry out for Pilate to crucify Jesus. Eventually He gave in to the demands of the Jews and "delivered Jesus over to their will" (Luke 23:25, ESV).

READ LUKE 23:32-49.

What did the soldiers inscribe above Jesus?

Jesus was crucified between two criminals. Describe the difference between how these men reacted to Jesus.

Criminal One (Luke 23:39)	Criminal Two (Luke 23:40-43)

In verses 44-46, Luke provided a detailed description of Jesus's death. Summarize what you learn below.

When Jesus died, darkness covered the land, a physical representation of the sorrow and pain that filled this moment. But right before Jesus spoke His final words, the curtain of the temple was torn in two. This curtain was the barrier between the holy place of the temple and the most holy place (Ex. 26:31-33), where on the Day of Atonement, the high priest would meet with God and offer sacrifice on behalf of the people. The tearing of the curtain was an announcement of sorts, showing that no longer did the high priest have to offer sacrifices for the people's sins because, by His death, the great High Priest Jesus provided a full and final covering for the sins of all humanity (Heb. 9–10).

READ LUKE 24:1-8.

Who went to Jesus's tomb?

What good news were they told once they arrived?

Crucifixion was a cruel and terrible mode of death in the Roman Empire. In the process, the victim was utterly degraded, "hanging naked to public view and suffering the jeers and taunts of passersby"; the cross was a "symbol of humiliation and agony."[15] But in Jesus's resurrection, this humiliation resulted in His glorification. Through His death and resurrection, Jesus accomplished four key things: (1) He conquered the power of sin and death (Col. 2:13-15; Heb. 2:9-15); (2) He made the way for the forgiveness of our sins (Rom. 3:21-26); (3) He fulfilled Old Testament prophecies (Isa. 53); (4) His bodily resurrection makes the way for our bodies to be resurrected (1 Cor. 15). With this one sacrificial act, Jesus accomplished His kingdom mission. In Genesis 3:15, God had promised He would fix what Adam and Eve's sinful decision destroyed. Through Jesus we see this promise fulfilled!

The kingdom of God is God's people in God's place under God's rule and blessing.[16] It includes a humanity living as sub-rulers, stewarding their divine identity and purpose for the flourishing of all humanity. The darkness of sin made this kingdom reality seemingly impossible. But with Jesus, the evil intruder has been vanquished, and peace and reconciliation with God have been achieved for all of humanity. Through Jesus, *shalom* is restored.

The King has risen and His rule has begun.

Hallelujah!

Day 5

WEEKLY REVIEW

This week we walked through our sixth session of the grand narrative of Scripture, where the promised King arrived and brought salvation to all humanity! Answer the following questions to summarize this week's main points. Feel free to use bullet points.

1. How many years were there between the last words of Malachi and Jesus's birth? How was He the fulfillment of the covenants God made with Abraham, Moses, and David?

2. Name some of the events that characterized Jesus's ministry.

3. What was Jesus's main message about the kingdom of God?

4. Why was Jesus arrested? Under what charges was He sentenced to die?

5. How did Jesus die, and why was the way He died particularly significant?

6. How does Jesus's resurrection fulfill God's promise of kingdom restoration?

SUMMARIZE THE NARRATIVE

In the space below, use your answers to the previous questions to create a two to three sentence summary of what happened this session in the grand narrative of Scripture.

Video + Group Guide

SESSION SIX

To access the video teaching sessions, use the instructions in the back of your Bible study book.

WATCH Session Six video teaching and take notes below.

DISCUSSION QUESTIONS

1   How are the Gospels the same but different?

2   Why did Jesus do miracles, and what does that have to do with us?

3   What was Jesus's relationship to the law?

4   How would you explain what it means to follow Jesus?

5   How did Jesus show that the promised King had come?

6   What is one point or truth that really stood out to you from the video teaching? Why?

THE STATUS OF THE KINGDOM

In the chart below, fill in the blanks to review the definition of the kingdom of God. (Look back at your notes on p. 13 if you need help). At the close of each teaching video, I will update the status of each phrase.

The Kingdom of God	The Arrival of the King
God's _____ in	
God's _____ under	
God's _____ and _____.	

SESSION SEVEN

The Kingdom Community

Timeline

SESSION SEVEN

JESUS'S ASCENSION

* Jesus appeared to His followers over a forty-day period between His resurrection and His ascension (Acts 1:3).

SAUL IS CONVERTED

AD 34

BOOKS

ACTS

ROMANS

1 & 2 CORINTHIANS

GALATIANS

EPHESIANS

PHILIPPIANS

COLOSSIANS

1 & 2 THESSALONIANS

1 & 2 TIMOTHY

TITUS

PHILEMON

HEBREWS

JAMES

1 & 2 PETER

1, 2 & 3 JOHN

JUDE

THE HOLY SPIRIT COMES AND THE CHURCH IS ESTABLISHED.

* The early church grew quickly, with three thousand added on Pentecost (Acts 2:41) and then another five thousand added not long after (Acts 4:4).

MEMORABLE WORDS

But you will receive power when the Holy Spirit has come on you, and you will be my witnesses in Jerusalem, in all Judea and Samaria, and to the ends of the earth.
Acts 1:8

As of 2022, Christianity is growing the fastest in Africa (2.77 percent growth) and Asia (1.50 percent).[2]

* Paul covered over ten thousand miles on three missionary journeys, making stops in three countries we know today as Greece, Turkey, and Syria.[1]

PAUL IS MARTYRED IN ROME

AD 47

AD 64

AD 70

PAUL TAKES THREE MISSIONARY JOURNEYS

TEMPLE IN JERUSALEM IS DESTROYED

* Saul's name was not changed to Paul when he met Christ. Dual names were common in that time period. Paul was his Roman name; Saul was his Hebrew name.[3]

MEMORABLE WORDS

There is salvation in no one else, for there is no other name under heaven given to people by which we must be saved.

Acts 4:12

Day 1

THE SPIRIT COMES

After this session, we only have one more session left! Do a little victory dance to celebrate all you have accomplished so far in this study. I'll be honest, as I was writing the last few lines of Day Four of the previous session, I got a little teary. No matter how many times I go through the story of Scripture, each time feels as fresh as the first one! Nothing compares to being reminded of what God has done for us through Jesus Christ. In Genesis, God promised He would permanently fix our sin problem, and through Jesus Christ, He did! The King has come!

This session we will continue the celebration of King Jesus by learning more about His kingdom community. By the power of the Holy Spirit, Jesus gathered a community of people, under His rule and blessing to continue His kingdom mission on earth.

READ ACTS 1:4-8.

What question did the disciples ask Jesus?

How did Jesus respond? What gift did He promise them, and what would be the result?

After Jesus's resurrection and before He ascended into heaven, He gave His disciples a kingdom assignment to tell the nations the good news that the promised king had come (Matt. 28:19-20). Through Him, the power of sin had been conquered and a way made for reconciliation with God. From Judea to the ends of the earth, Jesus's disciples would spend their lives inviting people to enter the kingdom community through faith in the King.

Following this commissioning, Jesus ascended into heaven to sit at the right hand of God the Father, sharing His throne and rule over all of creation (Phil. 2:6-11). For our sake, Jesus humbled Himself, putting on flesh to live, die, and be resurrected. Now, He has been exalted to the highest place of authority where He reigns over all of human life, all history, and all nations as Lord (Acts 2:36; Rom. 10:9; 1 Cor. 12:3).[1] But in His leaving, He did not abandon His followers; rather He sent a Helper who would empower them to fulfill His kingdom mission (John 16:7).

READ ACTS 2:1-13.

Who is the "they" Luke mentioned in Acts 2:1? What special festival had they come together to celebrate?

Summarize what happened in this passage.

What two reactions did the people in the crowd have to hearing different languages being spoken all at the same time?

1.

2.

In Scripture, Pentecost is also known as the Festival of Weeks (Lev. 23:15-21). Fifty days after Passover, the Jews would have a feast to celebrate the harvest. This feast was a time for Israel to bring the firstfruits of her harvest to God in anticipation of the whole crop that would be gathered. In God's divine timing, He used this moment to send the Holy Spirit to baptize and indwell His followers (Acts 1:4-5). The Spirit gave them the power to declare "the mighty works of God" (Acts 2:11, ESV) in the languages of a diverse group of people gathered for the Passover—Parthians, Medes, Elamites, Cretans, Arabs, and more. God's kingdom mission always included the nations, and at Pentecost, we see that confirmed! For Jesus's followers, the filling of the Holy Spirit marked a new season of ministry, when the King was dwelling with His people once again. And not only with them but in them!

Let's look at a Scripture passage to learn more about how the Holy Spirit equips the kingdom community to do the work of King Jesus.

READ JOHN 16:5-15.

In John 16:7, Jesus called the Holy Spirit the "Counselor." Compare this verse in the NIV and the NKJV translations. What word do they use for this name?

_____ (NIV)

_____ (NKJV)

Use the chart below to summarize Jesus's explanation of the Holy Spirit's work.

The Holy Spirit Will Convict the World About	Explanation

Based upon Jesus's words in verses 12-15, what will the Holy Spirit do for followers of Jesus? Where does He get His information from?

The Holy Spirit is the third person of the Trinity, sharing the same divine attributes as God the Father and Jesus, God the Son.

Sent by God the Father and Jesus, the Holy Spirit regenerates believers (John 3:1-8), giving us the faith to believe in the truth of the King and His kingdom. He produces in us the character of Christ (Gal. 5:22-23). He sanctifies believers, transforming our hearts to love what the King loves. This transformation empowers us to live out our divine design as image bearers and divine purpose as stewards of the King's kingdom. When we love what God loves, we can be focused on seeking the flourishing of all humanity as we fulfill the kingdom mission we have been given.

However, this kingdom mission isn't just for a certain group of people. God's mission has always included the nations, and in Acts, we'll see the disciples strive to make sure the good news about the King and His kingdom was made available to everyone.

READ ACTS 11:1-18.

In this passage, the terms *circumcision* and *uncircumcised* refer to different people groups. Match each term with the correct reference.

a. Circumcision (party)   The Gentiles (non-Jews)

b. Uncircumcised   The Jews

In one or two sentences, summarize Peter's dream and the message God gave him.

Whose house did Peter go to after his dream to share the gospel? Check the correct answer.

_____ The house of a Gentile (non-Jew)

_____ The house of a Jew

In what way did Peter's dream give him the approval he needed to make that trip?

Before Peter's dream, it was not a common practice for the Jewish believers to be in community with non-Jews (Gentiles). For so long, the Jews had been God's chosen people, which made their faith community exclusive. But with Peter's dream, God Himself showed that His gift of salvation is available for everyone—rich and poor, male and female, Judean and Samaritan, Jew and Gentile (Gal. 3:28).

So, fulfilling Jesus's words in Acts 1:8, Peter and the other apostles began to spread the gospel "to the ends of the earth." The tip of the spear in this mission was a man named Paul.

Paul (who was called by his Hebrew name, Saul, earlier in Acts) was a Pharisee and a persecutor of the church until he had a radical encounter with Christ on the road to Damascus (Acts 9). By the time we reach the end of the book of Acts, Paul managed to travel from Jerusalem, past Judea and Samaria, all the way to Rome, a fulfillment of the mission Jesus gave the disciples in Acts 1:8. Paul preached the gospel wherever he went. He shared the good news with people all across the Roman Empire, including Rome—almost two thousand four hundred miles from where he first met Jesus. In fact, Paul spent much of his after-conversion life traveling around the Mediterranean, planting several churches, and ministering to many more. Tomorrow we will walk through the letters he wrote to these churches and learn more about the birth and early years of the church, Jesus's kingdom community.

Day 2

IT'S ALL ABOUT JESUS

After Jesus ascended into heaven, He sent the Holy Spirit to indwell believers, forming the kingdom community. In Acts 2:42-47, Luke described how this community was characterized by self-sacrificial love, humility, and generosity—the very things Jesus taught and modeled during His ministry on earth. But as the community continued to grow, the need for continued support and encouragement became evident. Following Jesus is hard, and these first-century Christians needed help understanding how to live in allegiance to the King.

> **What do you find to be the most difficult thing about being a Jesus follower?**

The books of the Bible that follow Acts are split into two groups, the Pauline Epistles and the General Epistles. Both sets provide believers with wisdom, encouragement, and theological truth meant to keep them aligned to the gospel. In his epistles, Paul taught on the kingship of Christ and reminded believers of what it takes to access Christ's kingdom community. His teaching also helps believers understand how to live as citizens in the kingdom who are on mission for the King. The General Epistles focus on life in the kingdom community as well, with a focus on what it means to live in allegiance to the King in the last days.

For the next two days, we'll take a look at Paul's writings and then spend some time walking through the General Epistles on Day Four.

One of the main things Paul was concerned about was making sure the believers in these early churches had the correct understanding of Jesus. He knew they would be challenged by false teachers who would cast doubt on the nature and work of Christ. Let's look at some passages from Paul that solidify who Jesus was and is.

READ COLOSSIANS 1:15-23.

In the chart below, list what each verse says about who Christ is or what He accomplishes (or is accomplished through Him). Some verses may have both.

Passage	Who Christ Is	What Christ Does
Verse 15		
Verse 16		
Verse 17		
Verse 18		
Verse 19		
Verse 20		
Verse 22		

In this passage of Scripture, Paul gave us a beautiful picture of Christ. He detailed how He is the image of God, the firstborn over all creation, which means He shows us what God is like and is not a created being but is supreme over all creation. He stated that Christ has created all things and that everything in the world is held together by Him. He is the head of the church, this new kingdom community that is full of those who follow Him. By His resurrection, He proclaimed His glory and power because through Him God's plan of restoration is fulfilled.

Yet Scripture also shows us how Jesus did not use His divinity to gain or abuse power but to serve.

READ PHILIPPIANS 2:6-11 IN THE NLT.

Why didn't Jesus want to "cling" to His divine privileges? Does this mean He chose to stop being divine? Why or why not?

What word did Paul use to describe the position Jesus took on? How does this impact your view of Jesus?

To what extent did Jesus exhibit humility during His time on earth? How did God respond to this? Explain why.

In Philippians 2:5, Paul said our attitude should be the same as Jesus's. What would it look like for you to exhibit this same attitude with your family and friends? Give one example.

With much emphasis given to Christ's deity, Paul was reminding the kingdom community that the only king worthy of worship is King Jesus. In Paul's day, the world was overflowing with options for people and things to worship, especially in Roman culture. Caesar himself was considered Lord and demanded the worship of the people in his kingdom. But Jesus is greater than Caesar and the only One with supreme authority over the entire world. Yet the way He wielded His power is through service and humility, not domination. When Jesus left heaven to come to earth, He didn't leave His deity behind, but "he gave up his divine privileges" by taking on human form (Phil. 2:7, NLT). He left behind His position and rank and became as we are. He is fully God, fully man.

Paul was proclaiming this truth about Jesus's divinity to defend against false teachers that were trying to tell people Jesus was not God. Like a thread in a blanket, if/when the truth about Jesus's divine kingship becomes unraveled, everything else quickly unravels with it. Because if Jesus is not divine, our salvation is nonexistent, for no human has the power to overcome sin and death; only God can do that! In fact, the entirety of Paul's gospel message was grounded in Jesus Christ being God and King.

READ ROMANS 3:21-26.

What has God made possible for all of humanity? How?

How did Paul define sin in verse 23? What is the penalty for sin? Look up Romans 6:23 for help with your answer.

How does God's grace ensure we don't have to pay this penalty? What did Paul say will make us right with God?

Why is God's gift of salvation not based on one's obedience to the law? What makes this truth especially beneficial for Gentiles?

In Romans, Paul described how the law was beneficial. But the law was unable to deal with our sin problems; it only showed us how sinful we were. We are unable to obey God's commands perfectly (Rom. 7:7-25). This is the beauty of faith; it is a gracious gift of God. We don't earn it; it is given to us, and through faith, we can live in relationship with God as His people (Eph. 2:8) So now believers follow the commands of God out of gratitude, not obligation. In light of God's mercies, we live as transformed people who have been freed from the eternal penalty of sin!

READ 2 CORINTHIANS 5:17-21.

What do you think it means to be "in Christ" (v. 19)? Why does this position make us a "new creation" (v. 17)?

Look up the word *reconciliation* in a dictionary and then write a definition for it that fits its use in 2 Corinthians 5:18-19.

reconciliation

What responsibility do we now have as those who have been reconciled? Explain why.

Paul preached the message about the truth of the gospel repeatedly. In Romans 1–3, Paul drove home the reality that no one is deserving of God's gift of salvation. The penalty of sin is death, and as sinners, death is what we deserve. But Jesus paid the penalty for us through His death on the cross because God "made the one who did not know sin to be sin for us, so that in him we might become the righteousness of God" (2 Cor. 5:21). For us to be in Christ is to receive freedom from sin and gain righteousness that comes through faith. We are united with Him, cleansed from our sins, and made new. All because the King sacrificed His life for His people so that they might live!

The sacrifice of the King provided the way for the kingdom community to be formed. Sin led humanity to build its own kingdom, one that rivaled the kingdom of God. So sin didn't just make us bad people; it also placed us at odds with the King of the universe. However, Jesus's death and resurrection restored *shalom*, bringing back the peaceful relationship between God and man. And it is this gift of life that is the foundation for the ministry of those in the kingdom community.

Tomorrow, we will learn more from Paul about this ministry and what it means for us to fulfill the mission of the King.

Day 3

LIVING IN THE KINGDOM

Through his letters, Paul came alongside the believers in these early churches to help guide them through their spiritual journeys as members of the kingdom community. He wanted to remind them of their identity as God's people in God's place under God's rule and blessing. To do this, Paul used several metaphors to illustrate the significance of God dwelling with His people through the power of the Holy Spirit. This indwelling forms the basis for our view of who we are called to be and what we are called to do as the kingdom community. As co-rulers with the King, our mission is not just to spread the good news of the gospel with our words but to also proclaim the truth of its transformational power with our lives!

Let's look through some passages in which Paul unpacked what it means to be a part of the kingdom community.

READ 1 CORINTHIANS 3:16-17 AND EPHESIANS 2:19-22.

In these passages, what metaphor did Paul use to describe the kingdom community? Look up the word in a dictionary and write a definition for it that fits its context in the passage.

Based on your definition, what is the significance of the metaphor? (Hint: Think back to the building Solomon built for God in 1 Kings.)

READ 1 CORINTHIANS 12:12-31.

In this passage, what metaphor did Paul use to describe the kingdom community?

Using Paul's metaphor, explain how oneness and diversity work together in the kingdom community. Why is it vital that we pursue both?

The Holy Spirit gives each of us spiritual gifts to help us fulfill Jesus's kingdom mission. How does our pursuit of oneness help us not misuse our spiritual gifts?

The kingdom community is not just a social club; we are a global gathering of believers living to fulfill the mission of our King! We are the temple of God. He dwells in us by the Holy Spirit and works through us in this world. We are the body of Christ, with each of us gifted by the Spirit for the common good. But one of the major hurdles to our faithfulness as a corporate group of believers is disunity and spiritual immaturity. Paul knew this and used much of his writing to encourage believers to pursue spiritual fruitfulness. He knew that without it we wouldn't be able to fulfill the mission of the King.

For Paul, this spiritual fruitfulness came when believers walked worthy of the calling they had received (Eph. 4:1-5) and lived in light of God's mercy (Rom. 12:1-2). It was also connected to characteristics and behavior we intentionally choose to embody and practice, and those we don't.

READ COLOSSIANS 3:1-17.

In the chart below, list all the characteristics or behaviors associated with both the "old self"(who we are before Christ) and the "new self" (who we should be after Christ).

Old Self ("put to death")	New Self ("put on")

What type of mindset does Paul command us to have in verses 1-4? Explain why.

In verses 5-9, Paul shared two different lists of sins—characteristics and behaviors associated with the old self that we are to put away (or "put to death"). List the sins below.

The List of Sins in Verse 5	The List of Sins in Verse 8

What do they have in common? Look up 1 Corinthians 6:18, Galatians 5:19, and Ephesians 4:29,31 to help you with your answer.

In Colossians 3:12-14, Paul shared a list of virtues for the Colossian church to embody—characteristics and behaviors associated with the new self we are to put on. List them below and then describe what all of them have in common. What one virtue is elevated over all the others?

In verses 15-16, Paul gave two commands. Summarize them by filling in the blanks below.

"Let the _____ of Christ _____ in your hearts" (v. 15, ESV).

"Let the _____ of Christ _____ richly among you" (v. 16, CSB).

How does Paul's encouragement in verse 17 connect to what he previously told us to put on and put off in verses 1-16? (Hint: Note the categories of "word" and "deed.")

Paul's statement in verse 17 lets us know that the lists he gives for what we need to put on and put off are not exhaustive. As kingdom citizens, everything we do ultimately represents God, so we should live in such a way that consistently brings glory to our triune God!

In the words of Patrick Schreiner, "Christ shares his rule with his subjects and gives his Spirit to them so they can participate in his mission."[2] For us to share in His rule means that we live like the King, serving each other (Phil. 2:1-5), pursuing holiness and unity (Eph. 4:1-4), and embracing the road of suffering (Phil. 1:29). Paul's letters guided believers to order every area of their lives to live worthy of the gospel (Phil. 1:27), setting our minds on the King (Col. 3:2), bearing spiritual fruit (Col. 1:10), and denying the desires of our flesh (Gal. 5:24).

This internal transformation empowers us to pursue the mission of the King, making disciples (Matt. 28:19-20), proclaiming the gospel (Acts 1:8), and sacrificially loving our neighbors (1 Cor. 13) in such a way that they thrive.

This mission is the comprehensive work of *shalom* restoration, which is both spiritual and physical. Those in the kingdom community are not saved to wait for an escape from this world but to be witnesses to this world concerning the restoration of God's rule over all of creation.[3] I think this truth is captured well by this excerpt from a contemporary testimony called *Our World Belongs to God*.

Following the apostles, the church is sent—

Sent with the gospel of the kingdom

to make disciples of all nations,

to feed the hungry,

to proclaim the assurance that in the name of Christ

there is forgiveness of sin and new life

for all who repent and believe—

To tell the news that our world belongs to God.

In a world estranged from God,

Where millions face confusing choices,

this mission is central to our being,

for we announce the one name that saves. . . .

We rejoice that the Spirit is waking us to see

our mission in God's world.

The rule of Jesus Christ covers the whole world.

To follow this Lord is to serve him everywhere,

without fitting in,

as lights in the darkness,

as salt in a spoiling world.[4]

In the kingdom community we live to serve the King until He returns!

Day 4

LIVING IN THE LAST DAYS

We are living in the last days. Now, when I say this, I'm not trying to predict the return of Jesus. I'm just stating what the authors of the New Testament knew and the perspective they wrote from—we are living in-between the first and second comings of Jesus in a world desperate for the King to return. We "groan inwardly" (Rom. 8:23), expressing "our frustration with the sin that is so prevalent in our lives and in the world" and eagerly desiring for the glory of heaven to break into our reality right now.[5]

The authors of Hebrews, James, 1 and 2 Peter, and Jude all talked about the kingdom of God in a similar way as Paul—including a common focus on the reality of the kingdom community living in the last days. It can be frustrating to live in this in-between space and hard to not be overwhelmed by the weight of our spiritual waiting season. The authors of these books knew this and provided the kingdom community with an overflow of wisdom to help us live well as we wait.

The book of Hebrews was written to a group of Jewish Christians that were being tempted to walk away from their faith. The religious persecution they were experiencing was making them consider returning to their old ways of Judaism. The writer of Hebrews showed these Jewish Christians that, though they were faced with suffering, they were indeed following a better way—and they should persevere.[6]

Look up the passages listed in the following chart and match them to the answer that correctly indicates what the passage is saying Jesus is better than.

a. Hebrews 1:1-4   Jesus is a better High Priest.

b. Hebrews 3:1-3   Jesus provides a better covenant and sacrifice.

c. Hebrews 7:20-28   Jesus is better than the angels.

d. Hebrews 8:6   Jesus is better than Moses.

Since all of the comparison items are related to major tenets of Judaism, what is the overall message the author was trying to convey by using them?

SKIM THROUGH HEBREWS 11 AND THEN READ HEBREWS 12:1-2.

In light of the names listed in Hebrews 11, how might Hebrews 12:1-2 be an encouragement to Jewish believers who were considering turning away from their Christian faith?

LOOK BACK TO HEBREWS 10:23-24. What were these believers to do to encourage one another to "hold fast" to their faith (v. 23, ESV)?

Suffering is a real part of the Christian journey. We are not greater than our King, and if He walked the road of suffering, we will too. Yet amid those difficult situations, discouragement and doubt can quickly crowd our minds, making us vulnerable to hasty choices and wrong decisions. For example, when we believe God has forgotten us or that He won't be faithful to keep His promises, we can use coping mechanisms like shopping, overeating, or something even worse to soothe our pain. But all of these coping mechanisms are terribly insufficient to do what only God can do—heal our pain and sustain us amid our suffering.

As citizens of the kingdom of God and members of the kingdom community, "we are called to proclaim the gospel to a world that does not want to hear it and to live a Christian life among people who live in a very different way."[7] Ridicule, rejection, isolation, and persecution are all a part of the journey. But in these moments of suffering, we can look to the words of Hebrews that remind us that no matter what, life with King Jesus is better! He is the One we focus on as we model the same perseverance that was embodied by the saints of old.

READ JAMES 1:2-4.

According to James, how should believers view their trials?

What did he say our trials produce?

Throughout the rest of his book, James gave a series of commands, indicating the type of life believers should live, especially when they are experiencing trials.

Look up the verses below and write out the command or wise saying it contains.

Verse	Command/Wise Saying
James 1:5	
James 1:22	
James 2:1	
James 2:26	
James 4:10	

LOOK BACK TO JAMES 1:5. How does the wisdom God gives us help us do the commands/wise sayings you listed in the previous chart?

New life in the kingdom community means following the way of wisdom. But trials and hard seasons of life can lead us to walk away from this path and follow the way of folly, simply indulging the desires of our flesh. In these moments, James's words provide the guidance we need, like a light shining in the darkness. He shows us how true wisdom is displayed in us when we live lives where fighting does not define our relationships, where our words are used to heal and not divide, where no partiality is shown, where we are hearers and doers of the Word, and where we understand that the difficulties of this present life are preparing us for the life to come. In five short chapters, the book of James provides us with a rich perspective, full of insight that can help us navigate the in-between season of the last days.

Suffering takes on many forms, and the writers of 1 and 2 Peter and Jude knew that suffering by way of persecution was imminent for followers of Jesus. As believers live in a world that does not support or accept their religious beliefs, persecution will inevitably become a common experience. Knowing this, Peter and Jude wanted to prepare their readers to live with strength, alertness, and perspective as kingdom citizens who stood against the rival kingdoms of the world.

READ 1 PETER 2:9. What four phrases did Peter use to describe our new identity as members of the kingdom community?

1.

2.

3.

4.

READ 1 PETER 2:11. What two words did Peter use to describe those of us in the kingdom community?

1.

2.

How do the words and phrases of both verses 9 and 11 give you insight into who we are called to be as members of the kingdom community, citizens of the kingdom of God?

READ JUDE 3. Look up the word *contend* in a dictionary and write a definition for it below that fits its context in the verse.

contend

Based on your definition, what should we expect to experience as we fulfill the mission of God? Explain why. Look at Jude 4 for help with your answer.

Life in the last days will include suffering and trials, some brought on by opposition and false teaching. The letters of Peter and Jude provide insight into how we are supposed to navigate a world that is not just neutral to the message of the kingdom but stands against it. There will also be those who seek to deceive, proclaiming a message that is not the true message of the kingdom. So in order to contend for the faith, we have to know what we believe. The words of Jude challenge us to internalize the truth of the King's message so we can defend it and preserve its purity from those who will try to defile it.

The kingdom community dwells with the King, lives like the King, while executing the mission of the King. Who we are internally impacts the ministry we can do externally. Our ability to persevere on this side of eternity will be met with treasures in life everlasting. We are citizens of heaven who must, for the time being, live as "strangers and exiles" in the world (1 Pet. 2:11). But we shall not have to live away from home permanently. One day our King will return, and we will live with Him in a restored heaven and earth forever.[8]

Day 5

WEEKLY REVIEW

This week we walked through our seventh session of the grand narrative of Scripture, where we learned about the kingdom community. Answer the questions below to summarize this week's main points. Feel free to use bullet points.

1. What mission did Jesus give the disciples before He ascended into heaven (Matt. 28:19-20; Acts 1:8)? Whom did He send to help them with this mission?

2. What were the implications of the dream God gave Peter?

3. What type of work was Paul committed to?

4. What did Paul teach about the King and the requirements for entrance into the kingdom community?

5. What did Paul teach about the identity and purpose of the kingdom community?

6. How do the General Epistles help us better understand who we need to be as members of the kingdom community living in the last days?

SUMMARIZE THE NARRATIVE

In the space below, use your answers to the previous questions to create a two to three sentence summary of what happened this session in the grand narrative of Scripture.

Video + Group Guide

SESSION SEVEN

WATCH Session Seven video teaching and take notes below.

To access the video teaching sessions, use the instructions in the back of your Bible study book.

DISCUSSION QUESTIONS

1   How do the promises Jesus made to His followers before He ascended apply to us?

2   If you look at your church in light of the early church, how does it compare?

3   God has used the faithfulness of many people to get the gospel to you. Who are some of those people?

4   What is your favorite letter that Paul wrote? Why did you choose that one?

5   What does it mean to live our lives worthy of the gospel? Are you doing that? What is the evidence?

6   What is one point or truth that really stood out to you from the video teaching? Why?

THE STATUS OF THE KINGDOM

In the chart below, fill in the blanks to review the definition of the kingdom of God. (Look back at your notes on p. 13 if you need help). Then, at the close of each teaching video, I will update the status of each phrase.

The Kingdom of God	The Kingdom Community
God's _____ in	
God's _____ under	
God's _____ and _____.	

SESSION EIGHT

The Kingdom IS Restored

Timeline

SESSION EIGHT

JOHN RECEIVES REVELATION

COUNCIL OF NICAEA

FUN FACT

The Council of Nicaea was convened by the emperor Constantine to deal with the heresy of Arianism, a belief that Jesus was not divine but a created being.[3]

AD 90   AD 325   AD 1500

PROTESTANT REFORMATION

* John wrote Revelation from the island of Patmos (Rev. 1:9), an island off of modern-day Turkey that the Romans used as a penal colony.[1]

FUN FACT

The Protestant Reformation began in 1517 after Martin Luther published his 95 Theses. Legend has it he first nailed this document to the door of the Castle Church in Wittenberg, Germany.

BOOKS

REVELATION

* The book of Revelation gets its name from its first word, *apokalupsis*, which means to "unveil," "disclose," or "reveal."[2]

* The final battle is to take place at "Armageddon" (Rev. 16:16). However, there is no place named Armageddon in Israel. But there is a Mount Megiddo located in northern Israel. The Hebrew word for *mount* or *mountain* is *har*. Together you have *Har-meggido*, or Armageddon.[4]

I am the Alpha and the Omega, the first and the last, the beginning and the end.
Revelation 22:13

JESUS RETURNS/ FINAL BATTLE

NEW HEAVEN AND NEW EARTH

?

* When Jesus came the first time, He came as the Suffering Servant. When He returns, He'll come as a conquering King.

JUDGMENT

Then I heard a loud voice from the throne: Look, God's dwelling is with humanity, and he will live with them. They will be his peoples, and God himself will be with them and will be their God.
Revelation 21:3

* How many people have tried to predict the second coming of Jesus? Countless. How many have succeeded? Zero.

Day 1

THE SEVEN CHURCHES

For most of this study, we have spoken about past events. All of our discussions about the main supporting characters in the grand narrative of Scripture—Adam, Abraham, Moses, and David—referred to past events. Even in the last session, while we can glean much from the Pauline and General Epistles about what it means for us to be the kingdom community, the events that formed the community are in the past.

That changes this session.

The events we will talk about have yet to transpire (minus the letters to the churches in Rev. 1–3). Everything else is yet to come.

Friend, this is our last session together! Our quick race through the narrative of Scripture is about to come to an end, but we will end on a high note. You see, all the promises of God we've talked about—well, one last one is yet to be fulfilled. In John 14, Jesus promised to return, and when He does, God's plan of kingdom restoration will be complete.

Honestly, I'm tearing up (again) as I write this week. Because as Christians we believe our Savior King will return, our faith is grounded in Jesus returning and us living in a new creation with Him FOREVER. Just sit with that for a moment. We will live in a perfect world, without sin, with God, forever. And just in case you forgot, forever doesn't have an end date.

Before we jump into the lesson, I do want to give a brief intro to Revelation, the book we'll be studying this week. The genre of the writing is apocalyptic. This means that the writer, John, used symbolism to convey his message. Many of the symbols and metaphors he used point back to stories and prophecies from the Old Testament, especially from the books of Daniel, Ezekiel, and Isaiah. In the words of James K. A. Smith, "the point of apocalyptic literature is not prediction, but *unmasking*—unveiling the realities around us for what they really are."[1]

Like with all the other books of the Bible, we are not going to get into the nitty-gritty details of Revelation, but we will do our best to cover it at a fifty-thousand foot level. If along the journey you get lost, come back to these two reminders:

1. My friend and mentor Jen Wilkin often emphasizes the idea that "it cannot mean to us what it did not mean to them." Meaning: *Before we try to figure out what Revelation means for us in our day and time, we need to first figure out the message John was seeking to convey to his original audience.*

2. The key verse is Revelation 1:3 (ESV).

   Blessed is the one who reads aloud the words of this prophecy, and blessed are those who hear, and who keep what is written in it, for the time is near.

In the book of Revelation, John sought to encourage and challenge the believers to stay faithful. His message is grounded in (1) the spiritual reality of the cosmic battle; (2) the future hope of Jesus's final victory over sin, Satan, and death.

OK, that's it! Let's jump in!

READ REVELATION 1:1-9.

To whom does this revelation belong? How did John get a hold of it?

APOCALYPTIC literature is a genre of literature in Scripture that focuses on the future coming of Jesus and the final restoration of heaven and earth (e.g., eschatology). This genre often uses complex symbols and metaphors to convey its message and in Revelation heavily references Old Testament prophecies.

What two groups of people will be blessed by this revelation? Explain why.

1.

2.

What three groups of people did John send greetings from in Revelation 1:4-5? List their names and every title given to them.

1.

2.

3.

Whom was John worshiping in verse 6?

Where was John when he received this revelation? Why was he there?

John was exiled to the island of Patmos, probably because of his ministry endeavors. While there, he was greeted by an angel who gave him a vision from Jesus. In Revelation 1:12, John saw a mysterious vision of the risen Lord Jesus Christ. Jesus told John He had a message to send to seven churches and instructed John to write down and send out His words to them. Each of the letters had specific applications to those churches, but those churches were experiencing problems that our congregations are currently experiencing. So as you are skimming through the letters, note how Jesus's message provides timeless wisdom for churches today.

SKIM REVELATION 2–3.

John began his book by sharing Jesus's messages to seven churches. Fill in the chart below with the message Jesus gave to each church. (I gave you the church name and Scripture references for the first one as an example.)

Church Name	Commendation (if applicable)	Charge (if applicable)	Jesus's Instructions for the Church
Ephesus (2:1-7)			

Look back over the seven letters. What phrase is repeated toward the end of each letter?

"To the one who _____."

The same overall message is being conveyed in each letter—in light of persecution and opposition, God will triumph. Those who are faithful will share in the ultimate victory. Even though there might be uncertainty about the outcome of the battles they are fighting, Jesus is in control of everything happening in the world.[2] As Jesus addressed each of their strengths and weaknesses as a church, He also encouraged them to stay faithful. Those churches were acquainted with hardship, persecution, and the woes of living in the last days. And as the revelation unfolds, we'll come to see more about their motivation for faithfulness and the forces that were at work trying to make them stumble.

Day 2

WORSHIP THE KING

In Revelation, John pulled back the curtain and revealed to the seven churches, and us, the cosmic kingdom battle that has been waging since Satan's rebellion (Ezek. 28:12-18). Adam and Eve's decision to disobey God was an act of open rebellion against the King of creation. Their sin brought humanity into the cosmic war where the enemy's rival kingdom is warring against the kingdom of God. But even though we can often see the evidence of the war, many things are invisible to our human eyes. Revelation helps us see what has been shaping our world's history, a spiritual battle we cannot see from our earthbound and historically limited point of view (Eph. 6.12).[3]

In his Revelation, John saw a total of four different visions. Those visions were not necessarily linear but windows into the same series of events. It's as if each time John was showing us the events of history from a different perspective. The first vision was of the Son of Man and His words to the seven churches in Revelation 1:9–3:22.

We will cover his second vision today.

> **READ REVELATION 4:1-2.** Where was John transported to in this vision?

In chapter 4, John described a throne room that was an epic show of worship and adoration for our God. The vibrancy of John's words is breathtaking. The jeweled description of God, the twenty-four elders around the throne, winged creatures, thunder and lightning—all of this was a scene beyond words! John described how the elders and the four living creatures spend their time worshiping God on repeat. They don't stop. Day and night they continue to repeat the glorious truth about God and then fall before Him in worship, casting their crowns before Him. The twenty-four elders with their thrones and crowns seem to hold a level of power and authority themselves. But they cast it all before God to worship Him!

READ REVELATION 5:1-14.

Immediately after John's vision of worship, he saw a scroll with seven seals in the right hand of the One sitting on the throne. But there's a problem—no one was able to open the scroll!

How did John initially respond to this?

Who eventually steps up to open the scroll and break its seals? List His name and each title He is given.

Why is this person worthy to open the scroll (vv. 9-10)?

What was the response of those around the throne (vv. 12-14)?

How does this passage affect your view of Jesus? Your worship of Him?

The scroll John described in chapter 4 will dictate much of what we see come next in Revelation. The scroll itself represents sovereign control over the direction and goal of the history of the world.[4] But John wept because no one is worthy enough to open it. And then Jesus appears as a slaughtered Lamb, and He takes the scroll. Why is Jesus worthy? Because He gave His life to provide salvation for the world. As He opens the scroll, Jesus will be the One who will finish God's kingdom restoration plan.

READ REVELATION 6:1-17; 8:1-6; 16:1.

As Jesus opens the seals, who or what goes out? Here are the options you can choose from: a rider (list the color), death, or a natural disaster.

Seal One

Seal Two

Seal Three

Seal Four

Seal Five

Seal Six

Seal Seven

How many trumpets come after the seals?

How many bowls come after the trumpets?

The section of Revelation that starts the opening of the seals includes intricate, complicated, and confusing imagery. Without getting into the weeds with this passage, what we do know is that a cosmic battle is going on and will continue to go on. These verses show us how the kingdoms of this world are in opposition to the kingdom of God. At some point in the future, God will enact judgment on this rebellion. However, the seals, trumpets, and bowls are not describing three separate instances of judgment, but they all describe the same period of time.[5] The churches that John was writing to were experiencing opposition and persecution from Rome. So, through this part of his vision, John was reminding them that God saw their suffering and would bring about justice and victory! Nothing will thwart the things of God; His plan of kingdom restoration will be fulfilled.

What follows are several chapters that detail the spiritual cosmic war and God's judgment on humanity (which includes several opportunities for repentance). Then we arrive at the moment we are all waiting for—the King returns! But you'll have to wait until tomorrow to see what happens when He comes back.

Day 3

THE FINAL CHAPTER

Hope. This is what Revelation ultimately provides the seven churches and us.

It's easy to be overwhelmed at times by the hardships of life. If you add in the turmoil taking place in our nation and our world, our feelings of being overwhelmed can quickly turn into hopelessness. This leaves us wondering— *Has God forgotten us? Has He abandoned His kingdom mission? Is He really coming to restore the kingdom so that we can live with Him forever?*

The book of Revelation reminds us that God has not abandoned His mission and that one day the victory claimed by Jesus's death and resurrection will be felt permanently and holistically. *Shalom* will return in full, and we will reign with our Lord Jesus Christ forever! Hope wins!

But before we can have a full dance party to celebrate our forthcoming eternity with Jesus, we have to cover a few more events in God's kingdom plan.

When it comes to discussions about the end times, there tends to be a lot of debate about what will actually happen. But despite the difference in eschatological views, there are three key events that all Christians agree on—(1) Jesus Christ returns in a physical body; (2) the dead are resurrected; (3) believers and non-believers are judged.

Let's jump into the first event.

READ REVELATION 19:11-16.

When heaven opened, what and whom did John see?

How did John describe the rider? Who is with Him?

John used three verbs in verse 15 to describe what the rider will do. List them below. Are these actions directed toward believers or unbelievers? Explain your answer.

What name is written on the rider's robe and thigh?

Who is the rider?

How does this picture of Christ compare with what John wrote about in Revelation 5?

Jesus will return in power and strength and with an army! The King of creation will make the kind of entrance that Israel was hoping for when He first came to earth—not as a vulnerable baby, but as a mighty warrior who will crush the enemies of God.

The return of Jesus will not only be physical (John 14:3; Acts 1:11), but it will be sudden (Matt. 24:36-44) and glorious (Titus 2:11-13)! His return won't be a glorious experience for everyone, though. Before Jesus restores the kingdom, He will vanquish the enemies of God once and for all!

READ REVELATION 20:7-15.

The kingdoms of this world, led by Satan, go out to battle against the Lord. But does an actual battle take place? Why or why not?

Answer the following questions to summarize the judgment John described in verses 11-15.

Who is the judge?

Who is being judged, and what is the basis of their judgment?

Where do death and Hades and those not found in the book of life end up?

This passage mentions the book of life. Read the following verses and summarize to whom this book belongs and whose names are written in it.

Daniel 12:1; Philippians 4:3; Revelation 13:8

With God's judgment of creation complete, God's plan of salvation will be complete. Sin, evil, death, and Satan's schemes will be no more. The intruder is gone, and his control over humanity has been broken! The kingdom, God's divine plan by which He would dwell in perfect harmony with creation and humanity, can finally and fully be restored!

READ REVELATION 21:1-4.

What did John see first in this passage? What appears, and what disappeared?

What is the name of the holy city? Why is this name significant? (Hint: who else had a throne in a city with the same name?)

In verses 3-4, an announcement is made that gives the final update about the kingdom of God. Use the questions below to summarize this update.

Who are God's people?

Where is God's place?

Are the people under God's rule and blessing? If so, how?

READ REVELATION 21:22-27.

Why is there no longer a temple, a sun, or a moon?

What did John mean when he said, "its lamp is the Lamb" (v. 23)?

From what you read in these two passages in Revelation 21, describe what life in the holy city will be like.

Remember how I said the way the story begins matters? The Bible does not start with sin but with our triune God creating an earthly paradise so that He might dwell with His creation. And as we close this final page of the story, where do we end? In a paradise recreated by our triune God so that He might dwell with His creation forever.

Friend, this story is not a myth or a fable. It is the true story of the world. It gives us purpose, meaning, and value, answering all of our core life questions of identity, purpose, and belonging.

But for now, sin has not been permanently vanquished. We still live in a broken world. This means that the true story of the Bible is not the only story that you will be given the opportunity to believe and order your life by. Amid the noise of all those competing stories, I hope and pray you choose the only story that goes from beginning to forever.

A FINAL WORD FROM ELIZABETH

If you don't know Christ, I encourage you today to remember the truth about God's restoration plan and then spend a few moments responding to that truth. Specifically, remember God created you to live in perfect community with Him, following Him as our King. But because of sin we choose to live according to our own way (Rom. 3:23). Sin separates us from God, and we are powerless to overcome it. Even more so, because of God's holiness, the consequence of our sin is death. But in His grace, God sent His Son, Jesus Christ, to die for our sins (John 3:16). Through His death and resurrection, Jesus conquered the power of sin and reconciled our broken relationship with God. All we have to do is place our faith in Jesus, confess our sins, express our belief that Jesus is who He says He is, and commit to following Him as our Lord, Savior, and King.

(In this week of study, both Day 4 and Day 5 are used for review.)

Day 4

WEEKLY REVIEW

This week we walked through the final part of the grand narrative of Scripture where we learned about the return of the King and the final restoration of the kingdom! Answer the questions below to summarize this week's main points. Feel free to use bullet points.

1. What is the main message of Revelation?

2. Why is Jesus able to open the scroll? What does the scroll represent?

3. What do all the seals, trumpets, and bowls represent?

4. What two key events occur after the return of Christ?

5. What happens to the enemies of God, sin, death, and Satan?

6. What happens to the King and His kingdom community?

SUMMARIZE THE NARRATIVE

In the space below, use your answers to the previous questions to create a two to three sentence summary of what happened this session in the grand narrative of Scripture.

Day 5

STUDY REVIEW

Hey! We did it! We walked through the entire narrative of Scripture. Remember how I told you my goal was for you to be able to tell the story on your own? Well, this is when you get to do that. Look back over your summary sentences for each week and write them here. Feel free to edit and refine them to put them in story form. After you finish, you'll have written the entire story of Scripture in your own words. (Insert high five.)

Video + Group Guide

SESSION EIGHT

WATCH Session Eight video teaching and take notes below.

To access the video teaching sessions, use the instructions in the back of your Bible study book.

DISCUSSION QUESTIONS

1 When you read the book of Revelation, are you frightened, comforted, excited, or indifferent? Explain.

2 Do you ever struggle to stay faithful to the Lord? What encourages you to remain steadfast?

3 What do you most look forward to when you think of heaven and eternity?

4 What is one point or truth that really stood out to you from the video teaching? Why?

5 How has this study helped you to see that the Bible is one big story? Why is it important to understand that?

6 What is one thing you've really enjoyed about this study? What is one huge truth you're taking away from it?

THE STATUS OF THE KINGDOM

In the chart below, fill in the blanks to review the definition of the kingdom of God. (Look back at your notes on p. 13 if you need help). Then, at the close of each teaching video, I will update the status of each phrase.

The Kingdom of God	The Kingdom Is Restored
God's _____ in	
God's _____ under	
God's _____ and _____.	

Leader Guide

A WORD TO THE LEADER

Thanks for taking on the responsibility of leading your group! I know you will be blessed and challenged. Here are some tips to help you effectively lead the group study times.

FORMAT

Group Sessions
Each group session contains the following elements:

GATHER: This is a time to greet and welcome everyone and then to get them talking. In the first session, you're provided with some icebreaker questions. In the subsequent sessions, you'll use the review questions found on Day Five of each week to discuss the previous week's study. Feel free to adapt, skip, or add questions according to the needs of your group.

WATCH: Each time your group meets you'll show a teaching video. You can access the video content from the card in the back of your Bible study book. Encourage participants to take notes on the Video & Group Guide pages in their Bible study books.

DISCUSS: A list of questions is provided to help your group debrief what they heard during the video teaching. Feel free to adapt, skip, or add questions as needed to foster discussion.

CLOSE: You'll close each session by reviewing how they summarized the week of study and making sure they correctly filled in the Status of the Kingdom chart. Close the study with prayer.

Personal Study
Each session contains five days of personal study to help participants dig into God's Word for themselves. Encourage and challenge participants to complete each day of study but give grace to those who may not be able to.

Prepare
STUDY: Make sure you've watched the teaching video and completed each week's personal study before the group session. Review the discussion questions and consider how best to lead your group through this time.

PRAY: Set aside time each week to pray for yourself and each member of your group.

CONNECT: Find ways to interact and stay engaged with each member of your group throughout the study. Make use of social media, email, and handwritten notes to encourage them. Continue these connections even after the study ends.

SESSION ONE

1. Gather.
Welcome the participants to the Bible study and make sure everyone has a copy of the *From Beginning to Forever* Bible study book. Use the following questions to help your group get to know each other and get the discussion started.

- When did you first get introduced to the Bible?
- What would you say is the purpose of the Bible?
- If someone were to ask you to share the message of the Bible, what would you say?
- Why did you choose to do this Bible study, and what do you hope to get out of it?

2. Watch.
Watch the Session One teaching video. You can access the video by using the instructions in the back of your Bible study book. Encourage participants to take notes on the teaching session on page 12.

3. Discuss.
Use the questions and prompts on page 12 to discuss the Session One video teaching.

4. Close.
Take a few minutes to help your group familiarize themselves with the book, pointing out the different elements of the study. Make sure everyone finds the personal study they will complete this week. Then lead your group in prayer to close.

SESSION TWO

1. Gather.
Welcome your group to Session Two of *From Beginning to Forever*. Use the questions on page 36 to review the personal study for the previous week.

2. Watch.
Watch the Session Two teaching video. Encourage participants to take notes on page 38.

3. Discuss.
Use the questions and prompts on page 38 to discuss the Session Two video teaching.

4. Close.
Encourage some volunteers to share what they wrote under "Summarize the Narrative" on page 37. Also review the Status of the Kingdom chart on page 39 and make sure participants have filled it out correctly. Encourage your group to complete their personal study for the week. Close in prayer.

SESSION THREE

1. Gather.
Welcome your group to Session Three of *From Beginning to Forever*. Use the questions on page 64 to review the personal study for the previous week.

2. Watch.
Watch the Session Three teaching video. Encourage participants to take notes on page 66.

3. Discuss.
Use the questions and prompts on page 66 to discuss the Session Three video teaching.

4. Close.
Encourage some volunteers to share what they wrote under "Summarize the Narrative" on page 65. Also review the Status of the Kingdom chart on page 67 and make sure participants have filled it out correctly. Encourage your group to complete their personal study for the week. Close in prayer.

SESSION FOUR

1. Gather.
Welcome your group to Session Four of *From Beginning to Forever*. Use the questions on page 90 to review the personal study for the previous week.

2. Watch.
Watch the Session Four teaching video. Encourage participants to take notes on page 92.

3. Discuss.
Use the questions and prompts on page 92 to discuss the Session Four video teaching.

4. Close.
Encourage some volunteers to share what they wrote under "Summarize the Narrative" on page 91. Also review the Status of the Kingdom chart on page 93 and make sure participants have filled it out correctly. Encourage

your group to complete their personal study for the week. Close in prayer.

SESSION FIVE

1. Gather.
Welcome your group to Session Five of *From Beginning to Forever*. Use the questions on page 116 to review the personal study for the previous week.

2. Watch.
Watch the Session Five teaching video. Encourage participants to take notes on page 118.

3. Discuss.
Use the questions and prompts on page 118 to discuss the Session Four video teaching.

4. Close.
Encourage some volunteers to share what they wrote under "Summarize the Narrative" on page 117. Also review the Status of the Kingdom chart on page 119 and make sure participants have filled it out correctly. Encourage your group to complete their personal study for the week. Close in prayer.

SESSION SIX

1. Gather.
Welcome your group to Session Six of *From Beginning to Forever*. Use the questions on page 144 to review the personal study for the previous week.

2. Watch.
Watch the Session Six teaching video. Encourage participants to take notes on page 146.

3. Discuss.
Use the questions and prompts on page 146 to discuss the Session Six video teaching.

4. Close.
Encourage some volunteers to share what they wrote under "Summarize the Narrative" on page 145. Also review the Status of the Kingdom chart on page 147 and make sure participants have filled it out correctly. Encourage your group to complete their personal study for the week. Close in prayer.

SESSION SEVEN

1. Gather.
Welcome your group to Session Seven of *From Beginning to Forever*. Use the questions on page 172 to review the personal study for the previous week.

2. Watch.
Watch the Session Seven teaching video. Encourage participants to take notes on page 174.

3. Discuss.
Use the questions and prompts on page 174 to discuss the Session Seven video teaching.

4. Close.
Encourage some volunteers to share what they wrote under "Summarize the Narrative" on page 173. Also review the Status of the Kingdom chart on page 175 and make sure participants have filled it out correctly. Encourage your group to complete their personal study for the week. Close in prayer.

SESSION EIGHT

1. Gather.
Welcome your group to Session Eight of *From Beginning to Forever*. Use the questions on page 194 to review the personal study for the previous week.

2. Watch.
Watch the Session Eight teaching video. Encourage participants to take notes on page 198.

3. Discuss.
Use the questions and prompts on page 198 to discuss the Session Eight video teaching.

4. Close.
Encourage some volunteers to share what they wrote under "Summarize the Narrative" on page 195. Also review the Status of the Kingdom chart on page 199 and make sure participants have filled it out correctly. Encourage your group to complete their personal study for the week. Close in prayer.

ENDNOTES

A Word from the Author

1. Alister McGrath, *Narrative Apologetics* (Grand Rapids, MI: Baker Books, 2019), 9.

Session Two

Time line

1. "10 Remarkable Facts about Our Planet," Geneva College, April 21, 2017, https://www.geneva.edu/blog/uncategorized/earth-day-facts.

Personal Study

1. Barry Jones, *Dwell* (Downers Grove, IL: InterVarsity Press, 2014), 34–35.
2. Walter A. Elwell and Barry J. Beitzel, "Peace," *Baker Encyclopedia of the Bible* (Grand Rapids, MI: Baker Book House, 1988), 1,634.
3. Graeme Goldsworthy, *The Goldsworthy Trilogy*, (Milton Keynes, England: Paternoster, 2000), 54; Vaughan Roberts, *God's Big Picture* (Downers Grove, IL: InterVarsity Press, 2002), 22.
4. John Calvin, *Institutes of the Christian Religion*, ed. John T. McNeill, trans. Ford Lewis Battles, vol. 1, The Library of Christian Classics (Louisville, KY: Westminster John Knox Press, 2011), 37.
5. Michael D. Williams, *Far as the Curse Is Found*, (Phillipsburg, NJ: P&R Publishing, 2005), 41.
6. Thomas Schreiner, *The King in His Beauty*, (Grand Rapids, MI: Baker Academic, 2013), 3.
7. Stanley Grenz, *Theology for the Community of God*, (Grand Rapids, MI: Wm. B. Eerdmans Publishing Co., 2000), 174.
8. Tony Evans, Dan. 3:1–7, *The Tony Evans Bible Commentary* (Nashville, TN: Holman Bible Publishers, 2019).
9. Jones, *Dwell*, 41.
10. Williams, *Far as the Curse Is Found*, 65.
11. Mary Wiley, *Everyday Theology* (Nashville: Lifeway Press, 2019), 124.
12. Patrick Schreiner, *The Kingdom of God and The Glory of the Cross* (Wheaton, IL: Crossway, 2018), 32.
13. Williams, 85.
14. Ibid.

Session Three

Time line

1. Thomas V. Brisco, *Holman Bible Atlas*, Holman Reference (Nashville, TN: Broadman & Holman Publishers, 1998), 41.
2. *Ultimate Bible Dictionary* (Nashville, TN: Holman Bible Publishers, 2019).

3. "Twins peak with more born than ever before," BBC News, March 2021, https://www.bbc.com/news/health-56365422.

Personal Study

1. Chad Brand et al., eds., "Birthright," *Holman Illustrated Bible Dictionary* (Nashville, TN: Holman Bible Publishers, 2003), 220.
2. T. Schreiner, *The King in His Beauty*, 22.
3. Ibid., 27.
4. P. Schreiner, *The Kingdom of God and The Glory of the Cross*, 38.
5. Ibid.
6. Goldsworthy, 54; Roberts, 22.
7. P. Schreiner, 40.
8. Roberts, 78.

Session Four

Time line

1. "Overview: Judges," video, BibleProject, March 9, 2016, https://www.youtube.com/watch?v=kOYy8iCfIJ4.
2. "8 Oldest Monarchies in the World," Oldest.org, https://www.oldest.org/politics/monarchy/#:~:text=According%20to%20legend%2C%20the%20Imperial,What%20is%20this%3F/.

Personal Study

1. Holman Editorial Staff, *Ultimate Bible Dictionary* (Nashville: Holman Bible Publishers, 2019).
2. Roberts, 82.
3. Ibid., 84.
4. Craig G. Bartholomew and Michael W. Goheen, *The Drama of Scripture* (Grand Rapids: Baker Academic, 2014), 99.
5. Roberts, 86.
6. P. Schreiner, 79.
7. T. Schreiner, 193.
8. Bruce K. Waltke, *An Old Testament Theology* (Grand Rapids, MI: Zondervan, 2007), 760.
9. Chuck Swindoll, "Ezra," Insight for Living Ministries, https://insight.org/resources/bible/the-historical-books/ezra.
10. Tim Mackie and Whitney Woollard, "Esther: Secular or Sacred?" Bible Project, 2018, https://bibleproject.com/blog/esther-secular-sacred/.
11. T. Schreiner, 220.

Session Five

Time line

1. "Who are the authors of the book of Psalms?" Got Questions, https://www.gotquestions.org/Psalms-authors.html.

Personal Study

1. P. Schreiner, 68.
2. D.A. Carson, *The God Who Is There* (Grand Rapids: Baker Academic, 2010), 99.
3. P. Schreiner, 72.
4. Holman Editorial Staff, *Ultimate Bible Dictionary* (Nashville: Holman Bible Publishers, 2019).
5. J. Clinton McCann, "The Psalms as Instruction," Interpretation: A Journal of Bible and Theology, 1992, 123.
6. D. A. Carson, *The God Who Is There*, 97.
7. T. Schreiner, 300.
8. Ibid., 319.
9. Roberts, 94.
10. Williams, 191.
11. Ibid.
12. A great example of this is the story of Achan in Joshua 6–7.
13. Williams, 214.

Session Six

Time line

1. "Was Jesus born on December 25? Is December 25 Jesus' birthday?" Got Questions, https://www.gotquestions.org/December-25.html.
2. "Nazareth," New World Encyclopedia, https://www.newworldencyclopedia.org/entry/Nazareth.

Personal Study

1. As a fan of the band Journey, I couldn't resist writing that statement. You're welcome. :)
2. Bartholomew and Goheen, *The Drama of Scripture*, 134.
3. Ibid., 129, 131.
4. Ibid., 140.
5. Ibid., 141–143.
6. Ibid., 146.
7. Michael J. Wilkins, *Following The Master* (Grand Rapids: Zondervan,1992), 93
8. Bartholomew and Goheen, 144.
9. "Receiving the Kingdom Like a Child," Ligonier Ministries, https://www.ligonier.org/learn/devotionals/receiving-kingdom-child/.
10. Craig Blomberg, *Matthew, vol. 22, The New American Commentary* (Nashville: Broadman & Holman Publishers, 1992), 312–313.
11. Bartholomew and Goheen, 168.
12. Ibid., 168–169.
13. Gerhard Lohfink, *Jesus and Community* (Philadelphia: Fortress Press, 1984), 20.
14. Bartholomew and Goheen, 170.
15. Ibid., 176.
16. Goldsworthy, 54; Roberts, 22.

Session Seven

Time line

1. JesusFilm Project, "The Missionary Journeys of Paul," JesusFilm.org, February 25, 2019, https://www.jesusfilm.org/blog/paul-missionary-journeys/.
2. Aaron Earls, "7 Encouraging Trends of Global Christianity in 2022," Lifeway Research, January 3, 2022, https://research.lifeway.com/2022/01/31/7-encouraging-trends-of-global-christianity-in-2022/.
3. "When and why was Saul's name changed to Paul?" GotQuestions, https://www.gotquestions.org/Saul-Paul.html.

Personal Study

1. Bartholomew and Goheen, 187.
2. P. Schreiner, 112.
3. Bartholomew and Goheen, 216.
4. Contemporary Testimony Committee of the Christian Reformed Church, *Our World Belongs to God: A Contemporary Testimony* (Grand Rapids: CRC Publications, 1987), paragraphs 44-45.
5. Roberts, 142.
6. Chuck Swindoll, "Hebrews,"Insight for Living Ministries, https://insight.org/resources/bible/the-general-epistles/hebrews.
7. Roberts, 142.
8. Ibid.

Session Eight

Time line

1. "11 Things You Didn't Know About the Book of Revelation," BeliefNet, https://www.beliefnet.com/faiths/galleries/11-things-you-didnt-know-about-the-book-of-revelation.aspx.
2. *Ultimate Bible Dictionary*, 388.
3. The Editors of Encyclopaedia Britannica, "First Council of Nicaea," *Encyclopedia Britannica*, November 29, 2019, https://www.britannica.com/event/First-Council-of-Nicaea-325.
4. *Ultimate Bible Dictionary*, 292.

Personal Study

1. James K. A. Smith, *Desiring the Kingdom: Worship, Worldview, and Cultural Formation* (Grand Rapids, MI: Baker Academic, 2009), 92.
2. Bartholomew and Goheen, *Drama of Scripture*, 229.
3. Ibid.
4. Ibid.
5. Roberts, 150.

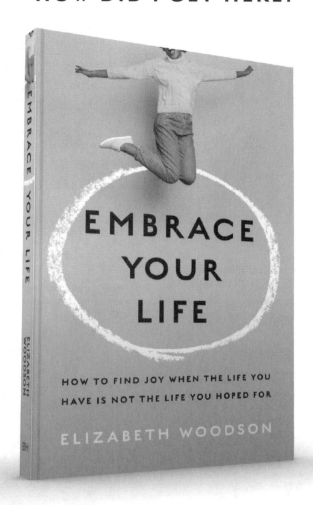

LET'S BE FRIENDS!

BLOG

We're here to help you grow in your faith, develop as a leader, and find encouragement as you go.

lifewaywomen.com

SOCIAL

Find inspiration in the in-between moments of life.

@lifewaywomen

NEWSLETTER

Be the first to hear about new studies, events, giveaways, and more by signing up.

lifeway.com/womensnews

APP

Download the Lifeway Women app for Bible study plans, online study groups, a prayer wall, and more!

 Google Play   App Store

Lifeway women

Get the most from your study.

IN THIS STUDY, YOU'LL:

- Recognize you are being formed by God's story.
- Come away with a greater understanding of who God is in every part.
- Cultivate a new framework/lens/perspective for future Bible study.

To enrich your study experience, consider the accompanying video teaching sessions, each approximately 15–35 minutes, from Elizabeth Woodson.

STUDYING ON YOUR OWN?

Watch Elizabeth Woodson's teaching sessions, available via redemption code for individual video-streaming access, printed in this Bible study book.

LEADING A GROUP?

Each group member will need a *From Beginning to Forever* Bible study book, which includes video access. Because all participants will have access to the video content, you can choose to watch the videos outside of your group meeting if desired. Or, if you're watching together and someone misses a group meeting, she'll have the flexibility to catch up! A DVD set is also available to purchase separately if desired.

Browse study formats, a free study sample, video clips, church promotional materials, and more at

lifeway.com/forever